Inclusion
and how to do it

Also available:

Inclusion and How to Do It: Secondary
Sue Briggs
1 84312 187 5

The SENCO Handbook (4th edition)
Liz Cowne
1 84312 031 3

Inclusion at the Crossroads
Michael Farrell
1 84312 118 2

Support Services and Mainstream Schools
Mike Blamires and John Moore
1 84312 063 1

Inclusion
and how to do it

Meeting SEN in Primary Classrooms

Sue Briggs

 **David Fulton** Publishers

David Fulton Publishers Ltd
The Chiswick Centre, 414 Chiswick High Road, London W4 5TF

www.fultonpublishers.co.uk

First published in Great Britain in 2005 by David Fulton Publishers

10 9 8 7 6 5 4 3 2 1

David Fulton Publishers is a division of Granada Learning Limited, part of ITV plc.

Note: The right of Sue Briggs to be identified as the author of this work has been asserted by her in accordance with the Copyright, Designs and Patents Act 1988.

British Library Cataloguing in Publication Data
A catalogue record for this book is available from the British Library.

ISBN 1 84312 351 7

Typeset by Kenneth Burnley, Wirral, Cheshire
Printed and bound in Great Britain

Contents

Contents of CD   vi

Acknowledgements   vii

Preface   ix

1   Inclusion in the primary context   1

2   Working with families   13

3   Planning and teaching for inclusion   30

4   Support for inclusion   51

5   Assessment to support inclusion: including the P scales   74

6   Want to play? Social interaction and behaviour   91

7   Communicating with children who have learning difficulties   111

8   Transitions: inclusion challenges and opportunities   133

    References and suggested further reading   147

    Index   149

Contents of CD

The accompanying CD contains many of the practical resources featured in the book, and some additional material. These may be amended/individualised and printed out for use by the purchaser.

Figures

Chapter 1
1.1   Education and associated services

Chapter 2
2.1   Respite care timeline
2.2   IEP review pupil comments form

Chapter 3
3.1   Pupil responses recording form
3.2   Tracking back diagram
3.3   Completed lesson differentiation planner and blank pro-forma
3.4   Concept map
3.5   Activity checklist
3.6   Example of a Clicker grid
3.7   Alternatives to writing
3.8   Observation form and tracking back grid

Chapter 4
4.1   Activity definition cards
4.2   What support might look like
4.3   Support record form
4.4   Peter's buddy timetable
4.5   Symbol of cat
4.6   Saw saw saw
4.7   *Handa's Surprise* symbols
4.8   Illustration of dog
4.9   Symbols
4.10 Symbols timetable
4.11 Communication board
4.12 Safety information
4.13 Example of memory mat
4.14 Signalong sign illustrations
4.15 Big Mack switch
4.16 Suggested contents of support toolbox

Chapter 5
5.1   Example of symbol-supported text, *Tumpa Tumpa*

Chapter 6
6.1   Completed grouping checklist
6.2   Blank grouping checklist
6.3   ABC behaviour observation form
6.4   Behaviour prompt cards
6.5   Feelings web

Chapter 7
7.1   Facial expression drawings
7.2   Ali's communication board
7.3   Self-assessment record
7.4   Self-reflection form
7.5   Symbol questionnaire
7.6   Happy and sad faces
7.7   Traffic lights template
7.8   Comic strip conversation
7.9   Draw and write technique
7.10 Cue cards
7.11 'Me' bubbles plus blank 'me' bubbles

Acknowledgements

I extend warm thanks to all those who through their constant support have informed this book with their experience and wisdom. Special thanks go to:

my critical friends, Bridget Jones and Sue Jones;

Giulia Lampugnani and the teachers of the Circolo G. Falcone in Pisa who challenged my assumptions and proved that inclusion works;

Linda Evans of David Fulton Publishers for her patient guidance;

my daughters for having unswerving faith in their mum;

my husband who has always supported this project with commitment and energy and blessed English skills;

my friends for listening.

The author and publisher acknowledge the following organisations for the use of illustrations within the book:

Widgit Software Ltd, Cambridge (www.widgit.com), for the use of symbols;

Gill and Mike Kennard of Signalong (www.signalong.org.uk) for the Signalong illustrations;

Crick Software Ltd (www.cricksoft.com) for the grid reproduced on p. 47. Reproduced by permission;

Liberator (www.liberator.co.uk) for the Big Mack figure on p. 71;

Phillippa Drakeford and Tony Maher for the cartoon illustrations;

Granada Learning Ltd for the *Tumpa Tumpa* illustration on p. 77.

To my beloved and loving husband

Preface

Primary schools are now welcoming pupils with a diverse range of abilities and individual needs. This book has been written for class teachers, SENCOs and teaching assistants in mainstream primary schools, and supports the inclusion of pupils with special needs, including those with severe, complex or profound and multiple learning difficulties. Advisory teachers and inspectors will also find the information valuable for their work in supporting schools.

Inclusion in the primary context

Inclusion looks different in every school. You need to find strategies that work in your classroom with your pupils. Inclusion is not a fixed state; it's a process that will take time to achieve. It is about continuous school improvement rather than a sudden change. Inclusion has to work for each teacher in each individual classroom. By finding out what works for you and ditching what does not, you can celebrate and enjoy the triumphs, and learn from strategies that turn out to be less successful. Teachers are not expected to put everything in place overnight, but to begin to look for new ways of including those children with a more diverse range of needs. The ideas and suggestions that follow come from many years of working with pupils with severe learning difficulties in special and mainstream schools.

Throughout this book the term 'pupils/children with learning difficulties' is used. A child has a learning difficulty if he or she:

- has a significantly greater difficulty in learning than the majority of children of the same age; or
- has a disability which prevents or hinders him/her from making use of educational facilities of a kind generally provided for children of the same age in schools within the area of the LEA; or
- is under five and falls within the definitions above or would do so if SEN provision was not made for the child. (Disability Rights Commission 2002)

The term 'parents' is used throughout and is also intended to cover any additional main care givers.

The legislative framework

New legislation introduced in September 2002 has brought about profound changes in the duties placed on schools. The SEN and Disability Act 2001, usually known as SENDA, amended Part 4 of the Disability Discrimination Act 1995 (DDA) to include schools and educational services.

'That won't apply to our school. We don't have any disabled pupils.'

Oh yes it will apply to your school! The duties are anticipatory in that they cover not only current pupils but also prospective ones. Schools are required to have accessibility plans that must address three elements of planned improvements in access for disabled pupils:

- improvements in access to the curriculum;
- improvements in provision of information for disabled pupils in a range of formats;
- physical improvements to increase access to education and associated services.

This book helps schools to meet the first two of these requirements by offering a range of practical strategies that will support access to the curriculum for pupils with learning difficulties and the provision of information in a range of formats.

The Act strengthens the right of parents of children with learning difficulties and other disabilities and special educational needs to choose a mainstream school placement for their child, so long as that is compatible with the efficient education of other children.

Won't including a child with learning difficulties mean more work for the teacher, leaving less time for the other pupils? Isn't that incompatible with the efficient education of other children?

There will be more work initially, especially in preparation and training, but once systems are set up, and providing the whole school is committed to inclusion, the child in a short time will become just another member of the class. Under the DDA, schools are required to make reasonable adjustments for children with a disability, and the preparation and training necessary to include a particular child would be part of that adjustment. Teachers and teaching assistants are enormously resourceful and creative people, with more skills and knowledge than even they realise. Children with learning difficulties are just that – children, with individual strengths, talents and needs. A colleague once commented, 'It's all a mind game really, isn't it, Sue?' And she was right; focus more on the child's abilities and less on the difficulties and you will find just how rewarding it can be to help the child to grow and develop as a member of the school community.

The new duties make it unlawful for responsible bodies to discriminate without justification against disabled pupils and prospective pupils in all aspects of school life. In maintained primary schools the responsible body is the governing body. The duties cover admissions, education and associated services, and exclusions.

What is the 'responsible body' for our primary school?

The 'responsible body' for a maintained school is usually the governing body. The responsible body is responsible, and ultimately liable, for the actions of all employees and anyone working with the authority of the school, such as contractors or parent helpers.

What is meant by education and associated services?

Pretty much everything that goes on in school is education or an associated service, including extra-curricular activities and school trips. Figure 1.1 gives schools an idea of the range of services covered by the Act, but this list is not exhaustive. Part 4 of the DDA does not cover other services that a school may provide to the public, such as a summer fête, or the PTA quiz evening. These activities are covered by Part 3 of the Act.

- preparation for entry to the school
- the curriculum
- teaching and learning
- classroom organisation
- timetabling
- grouping of pupils
- homework
- access to school facilities
- activities to supplement the curriculum, for example, a drama group visiting the school
- school sports
- breaks and lunchtimes
- the serving of school meals
- interaction with peers
- assessment and exam arrangements
- school discipline and sanctions
- exclusion procedures
- school clubs and activities
- school trips
- the school's arrangements for working with other agencies
- preparation of pupils for the next phase of education

(Disability Rights Commission: *Code of Practice for Schools* 2002:33)

FIGURE 1.1   Education and associated services

Will a school always know that a child is disabled?

It is not always obvious that a child has a disability. Such disabilities as Autistic Spectrum Disorder and dyslexia may not immediately be obvious. These, along with other 'hidden' disabilities, may take time before they are recognised and, if necessary, diagnosed by a doctor. Significant behaviour difficulties or under-achievement by children may relate to an underlying physical or mental impairment which amounts to a disability under the Act. A responsible body would have difficulty claiming not to have known about a disability if, on the basis of the child's behaviour or underachievement, it might reasonably have been expected to have known that a pupil was disabled (Disability Rights Commission 2002).

Section 1 of the Act defines 'a person with a disability' as: 'Someone who has a physical or mental impairment which has an effect on his or her ability to carry out normal day-to-day activities'. The effect must be:

- substantial (that is more than trivial);
- long-term (that is, has lasted or is likely to last for at least a year, or for the rest of the life of the person affected); and
- adverse. (Disability Rights Commission 2002)

Physical or mental impairment includes sensory impairments and also hidden impairments; for example, mental illness or mental health problems, learning difficulties, dyslexia and conditions such as diabetes or epilepsy. Also covered within the Act are people with severe disfigurements. The Disability Rights Commission (www.drc-gb.org) has published an excellent Code of Practice for Schools which contains useful case studies for staff training.

Not all children who have a disability also have special educational needs. An example would be a pupil with a physical disability but without any additional special educational needs.

Try to avoid making assumptions about children based on a diagnosis or other documents. Each child is different and will respond differently in various settings. By all means find out about the condition, but look at the disability in the context of the child as an individual. The social model of disability sees the environment as the principal disabling factor, as opposed to the medical model which focuses on in-person difficulties. Schools need to take an environment-interactive approach. Interventions should be centred on adapting the educational context, rather than on individual child characteristics. Chances of success are far greater where schools focus on adapting systems and curricula rather than trying to force a child to fit into the existing context.

A child with learning difficulties is likely to have a Statement of Special Educational Needs. The purpose of the statement is to inform teachers and to specify the provision needed by the child in order to meet their special educational needs. Part 3 of the statement details the special educational provision that the local education authority (LEA) considers necessary to meet the child's needs. The main objective in specifying that provision is to help the child to learn and develop. Part 3 includes objectives that the SEN provision in school must aim to meet. These objectives are an excellent starting point for setting Individual Education Plan (IEP) targets.

The *Index for Inclusion*

The *Index for Inclusion* (Booth *et al*. 2000) was distributed by the Department for Education and Skills to all maintained schools, but in many cases has been an underused resource. The *Index* supports schools in reviewing their policies, practices and procedures, and in developing a more inclusive approach.

The *Index* involves in the process all members of the school community as equal partners: governors, senior management, parents, pupils, teachers, support staff and the community. Partners are helped to identify areas for development through meetings and questionnaires. The *Index* gives a framework for developing an action plan, after investigating all aspects of school life, to make the school more inclusive. The process ensures that, by bringing the community together in this way, all have a stake in making the action plan successful. Schools that have used the *Index* have found the process challenging and sometimes uncomfortable, but the result is always valuable. Where it has been used as part of the school improvement process – looking at inclusion in the widest sense – it has been a great success.

The National Curriculum Inclusion Statement

The Inclusion Statement is part of the National Curriculum *Handbook for Primary Teachers in England* (DfEE 1999). It outlines how teachers can modify the National Curriculum programmes of study as necessary in order to provide all pupils with relevant and appropriately challenging work at each key stage.

The Inclusion Statement reaffirms that schools have a responsibility to provide a broad and balanced curriculum for all pupils, and that all pupils are entitled to the National Curriculum as the basis of the school curriculum. Schools are also able to provide other curricular and therapeutic opportunities (such as mobility training or physiotherapy) to meet individual needs *outside* the National Curriculum.

The statement sets out three key principles of inclusion:

- setting suitable learning challenges;
- responding to pupils' diverse learning needs; and
- overcoming potential barriers to learning for individuals and groups of pupils.

Setting suitable learning challenges

The National Curriculum programmes of study set out what pupils should be taught at each key stage, although teachers need to teach the knowledge, skills and understanding in ways that suit their own pupils' abilities (DfEE 1999). All pupils need to experience success and achieve their individual potential. Pupils with learning difficulties are no exception, even though their individual potential may be different from others of the same age. Expecting all pupils always to do the same work means that some will find the task too easy, whereas for some the challenge will be about right. There will still be a significant group in any class that will not understand the task, and which will fail. If failure occurs regularly pupils stop caring and begin to lack motivation, become disillusioned and are more likely to be disruptive. It is a teacher's responsibility to ensure that all pupils succeed, and a test of their professional skills is to modify activities and resources to that end.

Responding to pupils' diverse learning needs

Teachers will need to use a range of teaching strategies to match individual learning styles and employ a variety of activities within each lesson. To help pupils make progress it is possible to base work on objectives from earlier or later key stages. Particularly useful is the 'tracking back' method (see Chapter 3) which links age-appropriate activities to individually appropriate objectives. This method gives teachers the flexibility to devise interesting and challenging lessons that match the need for a greater degree of differentiation and for a more diverse group of pupils. The National Curriculum programmes of study that match pupils' chronological age can be used as *contexts* for learning and as starting points for planning learning experiences appropriate for a child's age and require-ments. It is especially important to have high expectations of pupils with severe learning difficulties. Such expectations will drive target setting for subjects and encourage pupils to achieve.

Each child brings to school his or her own individual strengths and interests which influence the way in which they learn (DfEE 1999). When planning for diversity, teachers need to be aware of the child's experiences and interests. Plan approaches that allow pupils to take a full and effective part in lessons. This will raise attainment for all the class and minimise disruptive behaviour.

What can teachers do to respond to pupils with such diverse learning needs?

- **Create effective learning environments that help children develop motivation and concentration**
  For some children this will mean devising a picture or symbol timetable, while other pupils may need an individual workstation in order to be able to concentrate on their own work.

- **Plan appropriate activities that allow all children to experience success**
  Design lessons that are interactive, and which involve exploration and sensory activities. Make sure all children are able to succeed at their own level. Ensure all pupils and staff respect the achievements of others.

- **Use a range of teaching strategies to match individual learning styles**
  Provide additional cues to help pupils who are not natural auditory learners. Use pictures, objects, concept maps or computer software to help all pupils understand and retain important information.

- **Manage support for pupils, both in terms of staff, other pupils and resources**
  Think *beyond* one-to-one support for children with learning difficulties, and investigate greater use of peer support or ICT. Adjust the style and level of support used so as to develop independence over time – a lessening of support can be one measure of progress.

- **Use appropriate assessment approaches, including the P scales**
  No more W or 'working towards'! The P scales now give a measure of attainment leading into Level 1 of the National Curriculum. Use photographs, videos and samples of work as evidence of experience and progress over time.

- **Set suitable and achievable targets for learning**
  Devise individual short-term targets that are challenging yet realistic. Avoid ephemeral objectives such as 'to improve understanding of basic mathematical concepts'. Set targets which children can aim at, and with which they are involved, such as 'I will learn to count up to five'. Share targets with pupils and parents, and give families strategies they can use at home to help children succeed in their objectives.

Overcoming barriers to learning and assessment

There are many events and conditions in pupils' lives that form barriers to their learning: hunger, emotional upset, illness, family breakdown, bereavement, etc. The barriers to learning for pupils with learning difficulties or a disability are usually very obvious. But some pupils may also be contending with additional barriers that may be less evident, such as hunger or a family crisis. Schools need to be sure that inflexible systems and policies do not create yet more barriers. Schools must take into account the type and extent of pupils' difficulties when planning the curriculum and assessment systems. For most pupils the need for curriculum access will be met through greater differentiation of tasks and materials. Some pupils with learning difficulties will need access to more specialist equipment or approaches. These may include developing the use of symbol systems, an electronic communication device or using materials and resources that pupils can access through sight, touch, sound, smell or taste.

What kind of action should my school take to help pupils overcome barriers to learning?

- Provide help with communication, language and literacy. For example, some pupils benefit from the use of key word signing to support communication. Investigate how software such as Clicker 5 (Crick Software (www.cricksoft. com)) can support literacy for individuals and groups. Use circle time to develop children's social use of language.
- Develop understanding through all children's available senses, such as providing visual cues in all lessons, or incorporating real-life artefacts and experiences. Don't just teach about plant growth; give children responsibilities to tend a small area of garden in the school grounds.
- Plan for full participation in learning and physical and practical activities; plan lessons in which all the class can be involved, rather than planning as an afterthought to include a child with learning difficulties.
- Help pupils manage their behaviour so that they may take part in learning effectively and safely. Structure lessons using picture or symbol schedules. Provide a 'chill out' mat or table in the classroom. Use social stories to prepare children for situations they find difficult.
- Help pupils manage their emotions, especially trauma and stress. Create opportunities for pupils to talk to a trusted adult or mentor. Teach the language of emotions. Use comic strip conversations and draw and write techniques, to help pupils learn *how* they can manage their emotions. (DfEE 1999)

The Inclusion Statement stresses that not all pupils with disabilities have special educational needs. For instance, a pupil with cerebral palsy may be very able academically but need a wheelchair for mobility. Teachers should plan to enable pupils with disabilities to participate as fully and effectively as possible. Potential areas of difficulty should, as far as possible, be identified and addressed at the outset without recourse to the formal provisions for disapplication from all or part of the National Curriculum.

Entitlement

Entitlement to the National Curriculum is very important for pupils with severe learning difficulties. Until 1944 these children were deemed to be ineducable, and came within the responsibility of the Health Service. Large numbers of children and adults with learning difficulties or disabilities were placed in long-stay hospitals and asylums. Children were separated from their families and local communities for years at a time. It was only in 1944 that local education authorities were required to find out which children in their area had special educational needs and to make appropriate provision for them. From 1944 to 1970, children with severe learning difficulties were placed in training centres rather than schools, and had no access to qualified teachers. The Education (Handicapped Children) Act of 1970 meant that for the first time all children with disabilities were brought within the framework of special education, with the entitlement to be taught by qualified teachers.

Those working in special education argued long and hard that special schools should be required to use the National Curriculum as the basis of the curriculum. It was feared that children with severe learning difficulties could easily be forgotten or marginalised, and that exclusion from the National Curriculum would be tantamount to exclusion from the education service (Mittler, in Fagg *et al.* 1990).

Inclusion as part of the school improvement process

All too often inclusion is thought to be synonymous with special educational needs, but inclusion is a much wider concept than that. Inclusion is about making schools more responsive to the diverse needs of individuals and groups of pupils; it is about improving the whole school from both an academic and the social point of view. When schools are really inclusive and more responsive to diverse needs, standards rise. A school that is good for pupils with learning difficulties is a good school for everyone.

Box 1.1	Clearing the ramp

A group of children is waiting to go into their classroom on a snowy morning. One of the children is in a wheelchair. The school caretaker is sweeping the steps. The child in the wheelchair asks, 'Please will you sweep the ramp?', to which the caretaker replies, 'All these other kids are waiting to use the stairs. When I get through shovelling them off, then I will clear the ramp for you.'

The child in the wheelchair then says, 'But if you sweep the ramp, we can all get in!'

Clearing a path for children with special needs clears the path for everyone (Giangreco 2000).

Inclusive ethos and values

The terms 'inclusive values' and 'inclusive ethos' are much bandied around in educational publications, not least by Ofsted, but these terms can mean different things. This book is about including children with learning difficulties and, in that context, an inclusive ethos has three important strands:

- **Belonging**
  A child's sense of belonging in the school community is a vital element of inclusion. Belonging is fostered by attitudes of staff and other pupils to individual difference and additional learning needs (Gray 2002).
- **Community**
  The school reflects and serves the local area, involves the people who live there and accepts as its own all children who live in that community.
- **Support**
  The whole-school community cares for and supports all pupils to enable them to succeed. This support is a natural and important component of working at or attending the school.

Where schools successfully include pupils with learning difficulties, the foundation of that success is the commitment of the head teacher and other senior staff to the broad principle of inclusion. The emphasis on inclusion is an impetus to raising standards for all pupils in the school (Ofsted 2003). This impetus is underpinned by a wholehearted determination from all staff to work for the greatest possible success for all, and a willingness to meet individual specific needs.

What will Ofsted inspectors look for in terms of inclusion?

As part of all inspections, Ofsted now looks at how a school's ethos tackles negative attitudes held towards people with special needs. Successful schools do this by celebrating and valuing the success of all pupils, fostering mutual respect and raising self-esteem. The words 'inclusive ethos' in the school mission statement is a start, but that ethos has to be embedded in the practice of everyone in the school – staff and pupils.

How can schools change attitudes and expectations?

We bring all kinds of past experiences, beliefs and values with us to work. It is just the same for people working in schools. For some the very concept of children with learning difficulties being taught in mainstream schools challenges the *status quo* and long-held beliefs and understandings. Teachers and teaching assistants can experience feelings of inadequacy in meeting these children's needs, and often have a fear of the unknown. Teachers tell of their concerns about keeping discipline, about not being able to communicate, about pupils' personal care and toileting, about medication, about epilepsy . . . about a pupil who is so 'different'. These worries are natural and understandable, but they are not reasons for *ex*clusion. All concerns can be addressed, and many problems resolved, before a pupil arrives by talking to parents and support services or by putting suitable training in place.

There have always been children with special needs in mainstream schools. Nowadays the difference is that many of the children have a wider range of special needs, and in some cases they may even look a little different. A pupil with Down's Syndrome can be more able than a child without such an obvious learning difficulty, yet a placement in a mainstream school may be questioned before the child's true ability is understood. Teachers need to look beyond the disability and see the real child inside. Focus on the child's learning strengths and needs rather than on a medical diagnosis, and use the diagnostic label as a signpost rather than as a dead end. These children have a great deal to offer our schools if we can learn how to recognise and celebrate their gifts.

Language and terminology

The whole area of special educational needs and disability is a minefield containing ever-changing acronyms and jargon: 'The SENCO and the EP liaised with a SALT about IEP targets for a pupil with an ASD.' These terms are a form of shorthand, useful for professionals. Used without care they can be intimidating for parents and irritating for some teachers. They do not make clear either the pupil's needs or the school's intentions. They may serve to exclude and alienate parents and carers, and can sometimes alienate professionals from other agencies.

The words we use when we talk about pupils with learning difficulties or a disability *do* have an impact on the pupils and how they themselves are perceived and treated. There is a useful rule of thumb when trying to decide what to say or write, which is to make sure the pupil is not defined by their disability or special need. In a sentence, put the pupil first and the disability or special need second, for example, 'a pupil with Down's Syndrome', rather than 'a Down's Syndrome pupil'.

Some words have negative connotations and are no longer in general use – a word such as 'handicapped' has its root in disabled people going 'cap in hand' for charity. Medical terms such as 'spastic', 'cretin' or 'cripple' were once commonly used to describe people with special needs or a disability but are now seen as inappropriate, particularly as they are often used as terms of abuse.

In general, the phrases 'a person with learning difficulties' or 'a person with special needs' are used, and this form of wording covers most eventualities. It is easy to become so interested in a pupil's particular syndrome that the child's individual personality is overlooked. A teacher once said in a meeting that his pupil was 'more David than Down's'. This meant that the child's character, individual experiences and support network were of far more importance than the medical diagnosis.

None of us is perfect; everyone is prone to a slip of the tongue, and it would be terrible if fear of using the wrong terminology discouraged adults from talking to or being involved with children with special educational needs or disabilities.

Training for staff and pupils

For many years there has been no specialist initial teacher training in special educational needs. All trainee teachers have some training for special needs, but this is often as little as a few hours of lectures as part of a one-year PGCE course. This level of knowledge does not prepare teachers adequately to work with the full range of pupils with special needs usually found in mainstream schools, nor those with severe and complex learning difficulties. It falls to local education authorities and schools themselves to arrange training for all staff.

If successful inclusion is to be achieved, careful preparation for admission should be started well before the pupil arrives. Teachers and teaching assistants need to have training on the particular needs of the pupils with learning difficulties who are to join the school community, and be given guidance on appropriate teaching methods, learning activities and specialist or adapted materials.

Training ought to be offered at a variety of levels. This should include:

- **training in disability awareness and the requirements of the Disability Discrimination Act 1995**
  This training will help staff to understand the issues relating to disability and diversity in society. It will support them in developing acceptance and an understanding of diversity among other pupils within the school. The Disability Rights Commission recommends suitable trainers. The cost may be shared if several schools train staff together, and this training may also be offered to pupils as part of a citizenship or PSHE programme.
- **general information for all staff, including non-teaching staff members**
  This will include an overview of the pupil's particular strengths and needs, the learning and behaviour strategies used in the child's current early years setting or school, and any relevant health and safety issues.

- **advice and guidance for subject teachers and teaching assistants on ways of differentiating and adapting lessons and resources**
  from LEA support and IT services, speech and language therapists, educational psychologists, physiotherapists and occupational therapists.
- **specialist training to address a pupil's specific needs**
  to teach staff how to sign, use symbols or a communication aid and/or administer medication.
- **ongoing opportunities**
  for meeting colleagues and the SENCO, the advisory teacher or the educational psychologist, and to discuss successful strategies and plan for the future.

Liaison with early years settings

This is an important aspect of the primary school's responsibilities, both in terms of general forward planning for all pupils, and where there are children with special educational needs. Regular meetings give a school several years of advance knowledge of potential pupils. This means that the issues of access, both physical access and access to the curriculum, can be addressed in good time. By using the same assessment criteria, such as the P scales, in both school and nursery, both establishments will gain a clear understanding of the needs of the child, and have a basis for individual education planning.

Welcoming pupils with learning difficulties

You can only make one *first* impression and, for children with learning difficulties and their parents, that first impression is especially important. Parents will be very sensitive to any negative comments or suggestions that their child might not fit in.

Comments such as:

'Have you visited the local special school? They have a wonderful hydrotherapy pool!'

'We are a high-achieving school'

'None of our teachers have specialist training'

'We can't take children until they are toilet trained'

may be meant well but do not make the child or the parents feel welcome, and in the case of the final comment, may be in violation of Part 4 of the Disability Discrimination Act 1995, if the reason the child is not toilet trained is related to his/her disability.

Just like all other parents, the parents of a child with learning difficulties will want to know that their child will be safe and happy in the school, and that staff members are friendly and approachable. A talk with the SENCO to find out about the SEN provision available for all children, and to discuss more individual issues, can follow at a later date.

Pupils with learning difficulties who attend mainstream schools are real pioneers – and so are their teachers and teaching assistants. You are all searching for an effective way forward. Give yourselves permission to make mistakes along the way – don't get downhearted and blame the child with learning difficulties for being there. Find a new strategy for one child and it will ease the way for another.

Not why, but how

Governments, at both national and local level, have made inclusion a political football. The reality is that these children now are in our mainstream primary schools. Recent legislation – and a forest of books – has addressed the 'why' question about inclusion. This book sets out to give schools some help with the 'how'.

Working with families

When a child has special educational needs or a disability, it is not only the child who is affected. To a greater or lesser extent all the family will feel the impact of the child's disability: parents, brothers and sisters, grandparents, even uncles, aunts and cousins. By the time a child starts school, the family has had four or five years of anxiety, challenges, and in many cases, grieving. Each family will respond to and cope with those experiences in different ways; some will be very angry; others may appear less concerned and get on with the job of raising their child, but that anxiety will still be there.

CASE STUDY	Jacob

Jacob is a much wanted second son. His mum had a normal pregnancy and delivery, and Jacob was an 'easy' baby for the first six weeks, rarely crying and seemingly content. Jacob sat at one year and walked at eighteen months. He was reluctant to eat solids and, when finally weaned, would eat only a limited range of foods, and although he showed affection towards his parents, he did not bring things to show them or point to interesting objects – he didn't share attention. At two years old, Jacob was diagnosed as having Autistic Spectrum Disorder (ASD). His family read all they could about ASD and in time they realised how severely affected he was by the condition. Jacob is a much loved son, but his family still feel the loss of the child they hoped he might have become.

Adding to the pressures and anxiety of having a child with learning difficulties, parents and families also have to deal with a deluge of professionals. They are required to take the child to frequent appointments, which sometimes involve long journeys. All these professionals are busy people, and parents often are reluctant to ask questions or seek clarification because they do not wish to take up valuable time. This can lead to misunderstandings and even more anxiety.

By the time the child reaches school age, parents may be wary of yet another tranche of professionals, this time from education. Each of these professionals will have their own area of expertise and have a different slant on the child's strengths and needs. Parents can feel that their voice is the least important and begin to lose confidence in their own ability to care for their child. Schools can ease this situation by listening and making sure that the opinions of parents are respected and valued as much as, or more than, those of professionals.

Supporting families through transition

The move from an early years setting to mainstream reception class can be just as daunting for the family as it is for the child. Early years settings provide an open, warm and supportive environment for children and parents alike. Some parents will need care and guidance to help them understand and be comfortable with the different expectations and routines of mainstream school.

Allow a parent to spend some time in the classroom before the child transfers, and go through the necessary documentation with them, such as the school prospectus or booklets about SEN provision. Have this vital information available in different formats, including on tape, for parents who experience difficulties with literacy. Information in other languages or access to an interpreter is necessary where English is not the home language, or in Braille should parents or other family members have a visual impairment.

Parents usually are delighted that their child has the opportunity to be educated alongside friends from nursery, but they will also have an additional anxiety as to how their child will manage in a mainstream class. Families' concerns are often not only about their child, but also about other children:

'How will they react to a child with learning difficulties in their class?'

'Will other children's work be disrupted?'

'Will the additional work for the teacher mean less time for the rest of the class?'

Parents may even be in conflict with other family members or friends over the decision to send their child to mainstream school. Inclusion is a relatively new concept, and grandparents and older family members may expect the child to be 'cared for' in a special school. These concerns can be assuaged if teachers and teaching assistants maintain an open and positive dialogue with parents and reassure the family that the child is an important and valued member of the class.

It is important to recognise the individuality of families and the uniqueness of the child. Schools must be flexible, respectful and non-judgemental in their dealings with families – whatever form they take (Carpenter, in Carpenter *et al.* 1996).

Parents as partners

As part of their mission statement, schools often state that they work in 'partnership with parents'. What does that mean in practice both for parents and for schools? With parents in general and with parents of children with SEN in particular, schools need to develop what the SEN Code of Practice calls a 'culture of cooperation' (DfES 2001). In order for partnership to have any meaning, schools must value parents' views, experience and expertise, and use parents' skills to complement and build upon what happens in the classroom. To acknowledge the parents' role as their child's prime educators is the first step in establishing a true partnership. The work of schools is more effective when parents are involved, and where account is taken of their feelings and unique perspectives. In practice this will mean:

- full parental involvement in planning the transition from early years setting into mainstream primary school;
- parents empowered and supported to take an active role in their child's education;
- parents helped to recognise and fulfil their responsibilities as well as to know their rights;
- schools listening and giving a positive response to parents' views;
- parents given access to appropriate information, advice and support, especially during assessments;
- sharing all information about a child with his or her parents in a 'user-friendly' way and language;
- the development of user-friendly procedures designed to engage and include all parents;
- sharing and acknowledging how parents and school staff feel about the child, and his or her placement. For example:

'I am anxious about meeting his needs' (teacher)

'We are hurt when other parents complain about our child' (parents)

'Seeing him make progress has been a real delight for me' (teaching assistant)

True partnership comes about through mutual respect and positive attitudes. Schools may need to offer additional support and encouragement to families with children with learning difficulties – to go 'the extra mile' to make the partnership work. It will be worth it.

Advice and guidance for parents

First time parents may be unsure how schools operate, and the expectations that teachers will have both of them and their child. Certainly they will need to be guided through the network of statutory requirements and responsibilities that go along with the education of a child with special educational needs or disability.

Much information will be given to parents when they visit the school for the first time, or at an open afternoon or evening. An additional and individual appointment with the head or SENCO will encourage the parents of a pupil with learning difficulties to ask questions pertinent to their child. This less formal situation will begin to build trust between parents and school.

Some parents may find it helpful to involve a third party, such as the Parent Partnership Officer, or a member of a parent support group. This outside person can act as a supporter for parents, and can mediate between home and school when parents are anxious or unsure, but this liaison should not get in the way of direct communication and co-operation.

Resolving disputes

As a child settles into the school, misunderstandings or disputes about provision or progress are less likely to occur where schools work closely with parents. It is when parents feel sidelined or patronised that problems start to build up, and it is then very difficult to regain lost confidence and trust.

When there is a breakdown in communication with parents, teachers at all costs should avoid the situation deteriorating into a 'them and us' scenario, with letters flying back and forth. Defuse the situation with a telephone call, or make a home visit to discuss a way forward, even if you agree to disagree. Disputes are like a virus that poisons all areas of the relationship between school and home. In the long run the child and his or her parents will still be a part of the school, and it is important that they are helped once again to feel part of that community.

Parental priorities – the long view

Primary schools care for and educate children for seven years. That is a long time, but only a small proportion of the child's whole life. Parents have a constant and continuing responsibility, and have to take a much longer view into the future, beyond even a time when they themselves will be able to care for their son or daughter. This concern is ever-present for families of children with SEN or disabilities, who would not wish siblings to have to take on the responsibility for their brother or sister. Because of this concern, parents are likely to have additional and sometimes different priorities from those of a school, often linked to life and independent 'survival' skills.

These priorities might be:

- basic skills: reading, writing and numeracy, so that the child will be able to sign their name, understand and fill in a form, or check their change in a shop;
- communication: being able to hold a conversation or ask for help;
- self help skills: being able to use the toilet and wash effectively;
- domestic skills: being able to cook a simple meal or keep a home clean;
- community or social skills: being able to behave appropriately in a café or supermarket;
- independence: being able to use public transport;
- safety: from exploitation, violence, or abuse.

In the primary phase of education many of these priorities will be addressed through the curriculum and PSHE. Other priorities will be covered as part of the parents' role in the day-to-day course of family life. When teachers talk about IEP targets in annual review meetings, parents will want to know how those targets impact on their own priorities. It is all very well Reshma learning how to 'generalise her communication skills into a variety of contexts', but parents need to be helped to understand just *how* a target such as this will help their child become independent in the future.

Open and relaxed dialogue between school and parents will ensure that parental priorities can be incorporated into individual education planning at times appropriate to the child's development. If this planning does not take place, duplication of effort will occur, leading to a waste of valuable time.

> **CASE STUDY**   **Ashok**
>
> Ashok is in Year 4 of his village primary school. Ashok has Down's Syndrome and associ-
> ated learning difficulties. Each Wednesday morning instead of maths, Ashok and his
> teaching assistant walk to the village post office where he is given some money and told to
> buy something – such as a book of stamps one week, a pack of envelopes another. They
> then walk back to school in time for play. At his annual review meeting Ashok's father
> asked the purpose of these visits to the post office. He was told that they were 'life skills'
> sessions. Dad then informed the school that Ashok went shopping with his family at least
> twice a week, often to the same post office, and that he had a weekly allowance, some of
> which he saved in his own bank account, and some of which is spent by Ashok, very
> sensibly, in various shops. Ashok would have gained more by being included in the maths
> lessons, where his understanding of numbers and money could have been developed to
> give him greater independence in the future.

Communicating with parents and other family members

Communication with parents of children with learning difficulties can be problematic. The children are usually transported to school by taxi or minibus, so
teachers do not have the opportunity to talk with parents informally at the start
or end of the school day. This situation makes written communication between
home and school even more important. Here are some ideas for moving beyond
the usual home–school books into other more creative and direct ways to
maintain close links with families.

Home–school books

Home–school books or diaries are the most common means of communication
between teachers and parents. They are a simple and effective means of exchang-
ing information but can be time-consuming at the end of a busy day. The
information is often rushed and sketchy, with a danger that the negative aspects
of the day are likely to be at the forefront of the teacher's mind. Where a child
has a learning difficulty or behaviour problems, the home–school book can
become little more than a catalogue of misdemeanours. Worse still, home–school
books are sometimes used as 'evidence' to try to obtain additional provision or a
different placement for a child. It must be soul-destroying for a parent to have to
read these messages every evening. Always try to balance the negative with more
positive messages, such as:

> 'Oscar sat quietly in assembly. He found the literacy task hard, but Mrs Jones
> helped him and he finished his work. A breakthrough in maths – Oscar
> counted to ten on his own for the first time. Oscar and James argued at
> dinner play so they both were sent inside to cool down, and they are now
> friends again. He made a sunset collage in art, and used the scissors very
> sensibly.'

Home–school books are most effective when parents are given copies of the class timetable and the medium-term planning at the start of each half term. Then parents know what lessons have taken place, and teachers need only give additional, important information. Don't worry if you cannot manage to write something every day. A full and informative comment once a week is preferable to a rushed daily scrawl.

Other methods of home–school communication

Communication folders

A communication folder is a simple, effective and fun way to encourage children to communicate about activities and interests in home and school. An A4 loose-leaf folder containing four clear plastic wallets is used. The parents and the child put items relating to weekend or evening activities into the plastic wallets. For example:

- a leaf from an autumn walk in the woods
- a burger wrapper from a fast food restaurant
- a train ticket
- the recipe of the buns made with granny.

In school the teacher opens the communication folder, takes out the item, and says to the child, 'Harry, tell me about this.' The item gives the child direct visual and tactile (and sometimes olfactory!) links to memory and encourages the child to communicate. Items can either be discarded or stuck into a 'news' book as the basis for a writing activity.

During the day the teacher or teaching assistant put items from school into the folder, such as:

- a picture the child has drawn
- a photograph of the child participating in an activity
- the conker found in the playground
- a photocopy of written work.

When the child gets home, the parents take out the items and say, 'Please tell me about this.' In this way parents have a much better idea of what the child has been doing in school, and this without the teacher or TA spending time writing in a home–school book. Stars, commendations, reminders, notes etc can also be put into the folder.

Email

Many classrooms now have email access. This is an excellent way to maintain and develop communication between home and school. A general class message can be sent out to all parents daily or weekly, with individual messages added where needed. Copies of schemes of work or lesson plans can be sent out which enable parents to reinforce concepts and support homework. Email is more informal than other written methods, and may be less threatening to some parents. Replying to email is also quick and easy and will encourage busy parents to respond – and an email can't be dropped in a puddle or eaten by next-door's dog!

Personal organisers and diaries

Personal organisers or diaries are a more age-appropriate method of communicating with parents of pupils in Years 5 and 6. A written comment or a sticky note attached to the page for the day gives the necessary information simply and discreetly. There is also the added benefit of including important dates to remind school, parents and pupil about hospital appointments, when items such as sports kits or musical instruments need to be brought to school, or when homework is due to be given in.

Dictaphones

Dictaphones are now relatively cheap; use them as an easy and time-efficient way to pass messages between home and school. Pupils love to use them, and for some children they can be a valuable motivator in developing speech.

Telephone calls

Some parents need an even more personal approach. When a pupil has worked well, tried hard or achieved a personal goal, a telephone call to the parents will be really appreciated. Build up direct positive contacts – this is a way of developing trust between school and parents and will make future problems easier to resolve. A phone call often sorts out minor misunderstandings, and is especially helpful to parents who may themselves have problems with reading and numeracy. A couple of timely calls may avoid a great deal of paperwork and acrimony.

Home visits

Home visits are the most effective way of developing positive communication with parents of pupils with learning difficulties. The visits should begin before the pupil starts school, and will need to continue for at least the first year. Parents will give teachers and teaching assistants the background to the child's learning and behaviour. This understanding informs target-setting, and makes Individual Education Plans more specific to the child's needs.

Meet the pupil in the home context, and this will have other benefits. Pupils are much more likely to be confident, happy and well behaved in class when they know their teachers and parents have close communication and are working together.

Sharing information

An open communication with parents also brings other benefits, especially when sharing information about the child. The more information a school has about a child the better able it will be to meet the child's particular educational and social needs.

Difficulties at home

Family crises are of course private matters, but schools need to be informed that the child may be experiencing anxiety or distress, even if details are kept confidential. Should a child's behaviour or mood in school change significantly, always contact parents first before putting into place any behaviour modification plan. The changes may not be linked to the child's learning difficulty, but could reflect a problem at home. Something as minor as mum being in bed with the flu for a few days can cause huge anxiety for a child, and where a child has limited speech, behaviour may be his/her only way of expressing distress.

Medical information

It is especially important for a school to have certain medical information when including pupils with learning difficulties. Any information will have to come from parents, and must be treated with sensitivity and confidentially. Once parents have shared this information the school can seek out any training necessary, and put systems in place for administering medication. When children receive all their medication at home, parents may not appreciate the importance of telling school about prescription changes, whereas changes in medication may have profound effects on concentration, learning and behaviour.

CASE STUDY	Kelly

Kelly is in Year 1 of her local primary school. She has a significant developmental delay and additional health and attention difficulties. Kelly's behaviour in school had improved dramatically over the previous term, but she also appeared lethargic much of the time and lunch time supervisors noticed that she had lost her appetite. Kelly's teacher rang her mum to ask if these changes were apparent at home, or if mum knew of a reason why Kelly's demeanour should have altered. Mum told the teacher that Kelly's medication had been changed following an appointment with the consultant. Mum had not realised that school would need to know about the medication change, and had assumed information of this kind would routinely be shared between professionals.

Absences

Pupils with learning difficulties, because of hospital or therapy appointments, or visits to specialist centres – such as for conductive education or assessment for communication aids – often have more absences from school. Inevitably, these absences will have an effect on the child's learning and progress. Wherever possible, consultations, assessments or therapy should take place in school. Many professionals welcome coming into school, as this arrangement offers them the chance to observe the child in the natural classroom setting, and to speak to the teachers and teaching assistants who work with the child.

Where absences cannot be avoided, for instance because of illness or important hospital appointments, teachers need to keep in touch with the family by phone or email. This will help the parents and the child feel they are still an important part of the school community. Sending home a short note, a couple of books or a game, lets parents know how much the school cares about them and their child, and reinforces the value of learning.

Links with parents' organisations and charities

Charities and parents' organisations, such as the National Autistic Society or the Down's Syndrome Association, are valuable sources of information and advice for schools. Often they produce excellent materials for schools on access to the curriculum, or on the management of medical issues. These organisations can also support schools more directly, such as advising on inclusive extra-curricular activities in which all pupils can participate, or delivering a series of workshops for parents, or assemblies for pupils; all of which increase awareness and understanding of particular disabilities among other parents and pupils.

Shared training

To meet the needs of a particular pupil schools need to arrange training on issues specific to that child. This training will always be more effective if parents are included, or even better are asked to be part of the training team. In this way 'everyone knows what everyone knows', and parents can be given an equal status alongside professionals. Parents are the prime care-giver and they really do know their child better than anyone else. That knowledge and expertise should be harnessed by the school as a vital resource.

What kind of training can be shared with, or led by, parents?

Health or therapy issues linked to particular disabilities or syndromes
For example:
- help for a child who has breathing difficulties;
- mobility exercises for a child with cerebral palsy;
- developing an occupational therapy programme in school, etc.

Classroom strategies to support a pupil with a learning difficulty or a sensory impairment
For example:
- positioning in class to maximise hearing or vision;
- structured teaching;
- support to enable the child to manage his own hearing aids;
- the use of ICT to support a child with a visual impairment, etc.

The administration of medication
For example:
- rectal diazepam;
- insulin injections;
- inhalers or nebulisers.

Shared training is a valuable route to greater understanding and co-operation between parents and school staff. It gives parents, teachers and teaching assistants time to focus on the child in a positive way, and sometimes leads to surprising realisations, as in the following example.

> **CASE STUDY** | **Johanna**
>
> Johanna is in Year 3. She has a developmental delay and health problems. Johanna has particular difficulties with maintaining attention, reading and writing. During staff training about Johanna's health problems, Mrs Carter, a teaching assistant, recounted an incident that had happened the day before. Johanna had asked, 'Where is the other Mrs Carter?' All had found this an amusing comment and carried on with the lesson. But Johanna's

mum was concerned by the comment and mentioned it to the paediatrician at the next appointment. The paediatrician arranged an appointment for Johanna at the eye hospital where it was found that she was experiencing double vision, and this was having an impact on her progress in reading and writing.

Respite care

Despite being very important to parents, the provision of respite care is very patchy across the country. Some parents may have as little as one 'tea time' each fortnight off, as relief from the responsibility of caring for a child with SEN or a disability. Schools need to be sensitive to the pressure this constant responsibility places on families, especially where there are other children, or in the case of a single parent.

Where respite care is a regular feature of a child's life it is beneficial for the school to have some communication with the respite carers, whether that care happens in a specialist centre or as a short-term foster care arrangement. Children may show their anxieties about transferring from one home setting to another through different behaviours in school. Communication between the respite carers and classroom staff, and the use of familiar systems and routines, will minimise these anxieties. Share with respite carers the child's individual education plan (IEP), individual behaviour plan (IBP) and any other strategies used in school – such as a few signs, symbol communication boards or a star chart for good behaviour. This continuity of approach will help the child to settle in the different environment, and better understand that they are cared for and safe in all settings.

The school must prepare the child for any changes to transport arrangements necessary because of respite care. A different driver or a change of escort can cause some children severe levels of anxiety, and lead to great upset and changes in behaviour. Give the child a favourite book or a toy to carry with them in the transport, a sort of 'respite treat' that will make the occasion more special and less scary. Tell the child how long it will be before he or she returns home. A timeline made of card and showing 'now' and 'then' will help the child to gauge how long they will be away, and to understand that they have not been abandoned for ever.

Monday	Tuesday	Wednesday	Thursday	Friday
Home	Claire's	Claire's	Claire's	Home

FIGURE 2.1 Respite care timeline

Life skills issues

Toileting

Some children with learning difficulties will enter primary school before they are completely toilet trained. This is not – and should not become – a big deal. The more anxious a child feels about toilet training, the longer it will take to happen. It is often the minutiae of a situation that cause most problems. Questions such as:

'Who should pay for the wet wipes to enable a pupil to clean himself independently?'

or:

'Is it OK for an adult go into the toilet cubicle with the child?'

are often stumbling blocks when these things should easily be discussed and sorted out with families.

When a child has particular long-term difficulties with using the toilet effectively, take a pragmatic approach and teach the child to be as independent as possible. Modern pads are easy to use, and most children quickly learn how to change themselves without help. They might need occasional support if they are ill or in a different setting, but this is equally true for young children without learning difficulties, many of whom also have accidents from time to time.

Modern pads keep children feeling dry and comfortable – perhaps too comfortable – and children with learning difficulties may not have the sensory awareness to know when (a) they need to go to the toilet and (b) they are wet. To help children develop this awareness, a short-term strategy is to put a pair of cotton pants *underneath* the pad next to the child's skin. When the child pees they then feel the wetness – linking the act of peeing to the sensation of wetness – so helping the child to understand when they need to go to the toilet.

Eating and drinking

Children with learning difficulties may have associated problems with eating and drinking.

These problems may take the form of:

- *Constant hunger*: where the child has no 'full up' sensation and so feels hungry all the time. Children with this difficulty are not just being greedy. Ask parents to put additional nutritious snacks into the child's lunchbox, especially foods that take longer to eat, such as an apple or a carrot. Frequent opportunities to eat small amounts of food will help the child to concentrate on work rather than on when they can next eat.
- *A restricted diet*: Most children go through a phase of being fussy eaters but some children with learning difficulties (and especially those children with Autistic Spectrum Disorder) will eat only a very restricted and repetitive diet. This diet may take the form of insisting on eating the same food for every meal, such as pizza or sausage and chips. This may not be a healthy diet but the child is likely to be getting most essential nutrients. It is when children

will eat only such foods as crisps or dry bread that long-term health concerns arise. This is a potential battle best left to families to resolve. In school, children should not be coerced into eating foods they find unpalatable as this could set up distressing negative connotations and could lead to the child refusing to come to school. If school is concerned about the child losing weight or appearing unwell, this should be raised with parents and mentioned to the school doctor.

Multi-agency involvement

Following the birth of a child with learning difficulties, the panoply of medical and social work professionals that opens up is daunting for any new parents. By the time the child starts school another swathe of education professionals will be added to the throng: portage workers, educational psychologists, LEA officers, teachers, teaching assistants. Listening to all these people, some of whom are eminent in their field, parents have to decide on the best course of action for their child. In particular, doctors often advise parents that placement in a special school would be best for a child. This is because doctors necessarily see the disability as the priority rather than the child as a whole and they may have little understanding of how a child with significant special educational needs can be educated successfully in a mainstream school.

Parents must be given the necessary information and advice, but all the agencies involved with a child must work together to give parents a coherent and thorough understanding of the child's needs. As far as possible, parents should be able to manage the process themselves and given copies of all reports so that they can read them in their own time and make decisions based on all the information available.

The language of reports

The professionals who make up multi-agency teams are all highly educated people, and each professional group has its own terminology and 'shorthand phrases' – or jargon. This jargon can carry over into the language used in meetings and in written reports. Comments such as:

> 'He has externalised his locus of control'

or

> 'She has delayed expressive and receptive language skills'

or

> 'By the end of Key Stage 1, we expect him to attain Level 2 in Handling Data'

may mean nothing to parents, nor most likely to the other professionals. Parents are entitled to both written and verbal information in a form they can easily understand. This also ensures that all professionals are able to work together more directly and effectively. This is not to recommend 'talking down' to parents, but endorses the sharing of clear and accurate information accessible to all.

Assessment/test results

The need for clarity also extends to sharing with parents test results or assessments. Professionals look at a series of figures and, through experience, can draw out the meaning and relevance – but parents cannot do this. A coherent summary of the results, written or spoken in plain language, allows parents to understand and ask questions. Important, potentially life-changing decisions often rest on test results, and parents deserve and should expect full understanding and involvement.

Collaboration with other professionals

A significant step forward can be made when all professionals work across disciplines, each accepting and respecting the expertise of the others and all working within a shared common concern for the child as a learner.

In this way team roles are not fixed, nor are there clear boundaries between disciplines.

For example, a speech and language therapist works in the classroom with a small group of pupils, including a pupil with learning difficulties, during a literacy lesson. This work is based on the objectives for the whole class, and the communication objectives from IEPs. The therapist also trains and monitors the work of those teaching assistants in the school who support children with speech and language difficulties. The programmes devised are based on and woven around the curriculum in the classroom, rather than being 'bolt-ons' that require children to be withdrawn. The therapist joins the weekly class team meeting and feels confident to make suggestions about learning that go beyond language and communication.

Other ways to develop collaboration across disciplines:

- a teacher working with a paediatrician to monitor the effects of a particular drug regime;
- speech and language therapists advising on the curriculum to promote a language-rich environment;
- occupational therapists advising on the furniture in classrooms, or having an input into the PE scheme of work;
- a team of teachers, social workers and workers from the Children and Adolescents Mental Health Service (CAMHS) collaborating on a social skills programme across the school;
- educational psychologists, teachers, speech and language therapists, occupational therapists and parents working together to devise an holistic programme of education and care for a child.

Decisions made by professionals collaborating at this 'shop floor' level help parents to see how everyone is working together in the best interest of the child.

IEP reviews

IEPs should be reviewed with parents at least every half term in the child's infant phase. At this age children's strengths and needs can change very quickly. Termly reviews will be more appropriate as the child gets older. Review meetings are only as good as the IEP; if the targets are imprecise the discussion will not be focused and the meeting will take longer. Go through each target one by one, then ask parents if there is anything else related to the IEP that they would like to discuss. Look at the progress made by the child from the point of view of the school, the parents and the child.

Some parents find it helpful to have a comments sheet to fill in before the meeting. This helps them to remember to ask the questions that they feel are important, rather than their fitting to the school's agenda. A pupil comments sheet is also valuable if the child is not to attend the meeting. This can be a fun and valuable way for the child to reflect on their progress against the IEP targets, and may be used to record attainment.

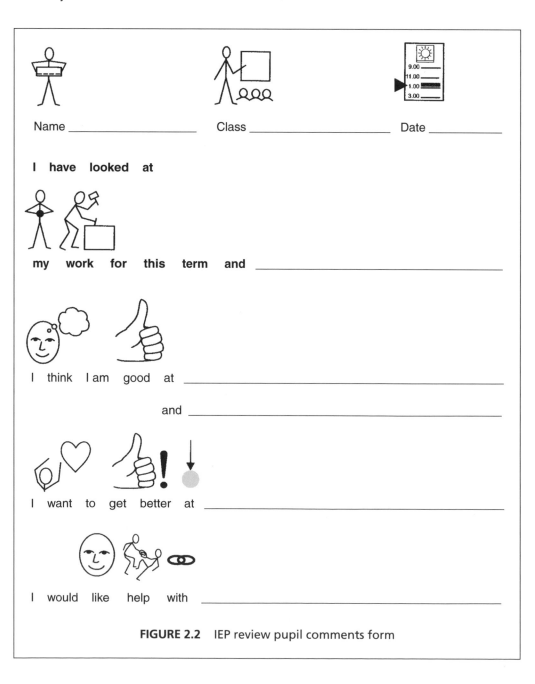

FIGURE 2.2 IEP review pupil comments form

The effectiveness of the IEP should also be evaluated. If the pupil is not making the progress expected by any of the stakeholders, perhaps either the targets are not appropriate or the support given is not effective. Any specific difficulties that impact on the child's learning should be discussed, such as problems with physical access or accessing the curriculum. New targets and future action can be agreed at the meeting, with the roles of parents, school and the child clearly set out.

Framework for the meeting

1. Progress:
   - Parents' view:
   - School's view:
   - Pupil's view:
2. Effectiveness of the IEP
3. Specific measures to be taken to ensure access
4. Updated information and/or advice
5. New targets and responsibilities
6. Any other questions.

Annual review meetings

LEAs have a statutory duty to arrange annual meetings to review a child's Statement of Special Educational Needs. The annual review ensures that once a year the parents, the child, the LEA, the school and all the professionals involved consider the progress the pupil has made over the previous year, and whether amendments need to be made to the description of the child's needs or to the special educational provision specified in the statement (DfES 2001). The statement should be at the heart of this meeting and all those present must have a copy. This meeting is separate from the review of the child's IEP, although objectives will be set for the following year on which IEP targets will be based.

Parents, and all the professionals involved with the pupil, will be invited both to send a report and to attend the meeting. Parents new to the annual review system may expect all the professionals from outside the school to attend the meeting, and can be very disappointed when they find it is just themselves and school staff. Let parents know in advance that professionals from outside school, such as educational psychologists or occupational therapists, usually only attend annual reviews before major transitions, or if significant changes are to be made to provision.

When a large number of professionals are to attend the meeting, make sure parents know well in advance exactly who will be there, and who will be chairing the meeting. Offer a pre-meeting between the parents and SENCO or the class teacher, so that together they can prepare any questions. Difficult issues, such as whether parents wish the child to attend the meeting, can be raised and discussed in this more informal setting. Allow parents to bring a friend or family member to give support at the meeting. This is especially important for a single parent, or if only one parent is able to attend.

Effective communication between home and school should mean that there are no surprises for parents at this meeting. Any potentially distressing or difficult information should be given to parents and explained before the meeting.

It is useful to send out a simple agenda at least a week before the meeting. This should list the issues to be discussed so that parents know what is going to happen, and when.

At the meeting:

- The chair should introduce the parents and then ask each of the professionals to introduce themselves, explaining their role and the reason for their being at the meeting.
- If the child is not to attend the meeting, place a photograph of him or her in the middle of the table. This keeps the child at the forefront of the discussion. Written or taped comments from the child, even pictures they have drawn about school, can be used to present their perspective.
- Always invite parents to speak first at the start of the meeting, and allow them the final word at the end. If parents are reluctant to speak, encourage them gently as they must feel they have had their say. If not, they are likely to become disillusioned and negative.
- No new diagnoses, test results or major changes to provision should ever be brought up in annual review meetings without parents being given this information privately beforehand. Sudden revelations are unfair to parents and will ruin any trust built up over time. If communication between home and school is working as it should, the meeting should simply build on and consolidate information already shared and discussed.

Pastoral support

Parents will be very interested in the pastoral support that the school can offer their child; indeed this is often a major factor in determining a family's choice of school. Some children with learning difficulties are amazingly resilient and require very little additional support. Others will need a high level of pastoral care, both from school professionals and outside agencies, such as educational psychology or CAMHS.

Working with siblings

The siblings of children with learning difficulties will each have their own ways of coming to terms with having a brother or sister who has a learning difficulty. Having a sibling with learning difficulties in the same school should not in itself make the situation more difficult, although some parents do prefer their children to be in different schools. This is usually because parents fear that the sibling might feel they have to take responsibility for a sister or brother with learning difficulties. Schools do have to be cautious neither to expect nor to allow siblings to take on this responsibility; they should be treated just the same as all other brothers and sisters would be in school.

There will inevitably be comparisons between siblings. A much younger child might outstrip their big brother or sister academically, and the child with learning difficulties may lose self-esteem and their role as older sibling. Where this is the case, endeavour to boost the status of the older child within the school by giving responsibilities or praising other skills and qualities, such as being a good friend.

Older sisters and brothers must be allowed the freedom to develop in their own right and not just as James' or Joanna's brother. Some children will have a great sense of responsibility towards their brother or sister, and school will need to watch that the sibling does not take on the role of minder. Other children will make every effort to have no contact with their siblings in school time.

A strong and trusting ongoing relationship with parents will be a huge bonus for the whole family should the child with learning difficulties become ill or develop a secondary condition such as epilepsy. During periods of illness the parents must focus on the sick child, and other children may be worried about their sibling but might also feel left out. Teachers and teaching assistants can help through these times by giving the children opportunities to talk about the situation at home in a relaxed and informal way. Children can carry a huge amount of anxiety, often thinking that they might be to blame in some way, and a quiet chat during a play session can ease that burden.

Summary

Parents are the real experts about their own children. When the professionals have gone home at the end of the day, parents once again take on that life-long responsibility.

Working with parents brings benefits for children and for the school. A teacher or teaching assistant in a primary school is a very important part of a child's life for a year, and your actions and opinions will affect the child's whole family. Keep the channels of communication open, especially during difficult periods or disagreement, and you can share all the challenges and successes, and feel less anxious about meeting the child's needs.

Chapter 3 gives teachers advice and support for planning the inclusive curriculum.

3 Planning and teaching for inclusion

The foundation stage

Children enter school with a broad diversity in terms of development, experience, interests and skills; and now part of that mainstream spectrum are children with more significant special educational needs and disabilities.

The foundation stage in the reception class is usually considered to be less problematic in planning to include pupils with learning difficulties. The child's needs for play and interaction with others are the same as those of all children entering school for the first time. The basis of the foundation stage curriculum in play and exploration is ideal for pupils with special educational needs and disabilities. However, there are certain challenges at this stage which can be addressed through careful planning and adaptation of the curriculum.

The child's early years setting will have passed on information about how the child has been included and his/her areas of relative strength and priorities for development. This information, in addition to discussion with parents and carers, forms a firm basis for planning the curriculum to meet the needs of the child with learning difficulties.

Planning is most effective when teachers start with children with learning difficulties in mind, where they are at the hub of the planning. This ensures the activities will be truly inclusive and meet the needs of all the class. It is much simpler then to extend tasks or activities for more able pupils, than it is later to adapt activities for pupils with learning difficulties.

At this young age children with learning difficulties will not be able to sustain attention for long periods. Initially, activities should be:

- *Short*: Match the length of the task or activity to the child's ability to attend or concentrate.
- *Focused*: Offer one task at a time on a clear table. Other objects – even the teacher's pen – will deflect the child's attention.
- *Varied*: Maintain a balance throughout each session between table activities and play that involves more boisterous movement.
- *Sensory*: Harness all sensory experience to maximise learning through touch, taste and smell, as well as sight and sound. Children with learning difficulties usually are much stronger visually than aurally. Linking sounds with a visual stimulus – such as a sign or a symbol – will increase the impact of learning. The sense of smell is closely linked to memory, so linking pleasant smells to experiences will help the child bring the occasion to mind at a later time.

■ **Balanced**: Children in the foundation stage with SEN and disabilities often need to learn how to interact with adults and with other children. Build in time for the child to play alone, with an adult, with one other child, and as part of a group. Even if the child has one-to-one support, this balance of interaction remains of vital importance.

■ **Flexible**: Don't flog a dead horse! Sometimes children with learning difficulties cannot settle to a particular task or type of activity. The child may need to spend extra time outdoors, or just curled up on a bean bag with a book. This isn't to say that a child should 'get away with' not participating just because of his or her learning difficulty, more that the adults working with him/her need to be sensitive to the child's particular needs.

For children with learning difficulties tiredness is a significant factor. Build regular rest, or 'down times', into the child's schedule. Children may not always sleep, but they will need more opportunities for additional quiet time alone, or for listening to a story tape.

As attention and concentration develop, the length and complexity of activities can be increased. Always be guided by the child rather than forcing the pace. Putting a child under pressure causes anxiety that leads to the child either becoming withdrawn or to challenging behaviour.

To move up or not to move up?

Schools can be tempted to leave a child in reception class for an additional year – or even longer – as the curriculum and atmosphere in the reception class may seem more appropriate for the child's learning and social needs. This may appear to be a neat solution, but merely stores up difficulties for later. Children have to move on to the next phase of education at set ages, and so will have to 'catch up' with their chronological age group at some point. Keeping pupils with their chronological peers helps them to learn age-appropriate behaviour and ensures they receive the broad and balanced curriculum to which they are entitled. This book gives guidance on how teachers throughout the school can differentiate their lessons to meet a more diverse range of abilities.

Planning the curriculum for inclusion in the primary curriculum

In any mainstream year group there will always be several pupils operating at earlier or later National Curriculum levels than the majority of their peers. This chapter will give teachers ideas on how to make the primary curriculum more inclusive for pupils with learning difficulties without creating a mountain of extra work.

Planning for classes that include pupils with learning difficulties is sometimes daunting and teachers can be put off even before they start. It really doesn't have to be complicated, nor need it create a great deal of additional work. The key is to avoid creating a completely different curriculum for one pupil; you can adapt the planning systems you have already. However, planning for pupils with learning difficulties is impossible to do 'on the hoof'; it needs to be done in advance, at the same time as the planning for the rest of the group. Keep an extra piece of paper on the side of the desk and as opportunities for differentiation arise, write them down.

New learning should be teacher-led, with teaching assistants supporting pupils in practising and consolidating the skills and knowledge.

It is vital to have high expectations of all pupils even, or especially, for those with learning difficulties.

From the outset it is important to say that it is not up to a child with a learning disability to cope with the curriculum. It is up to schools and teachers to adapt the curriculum, and their teaching styles, to meet the needs of the individual pupil. Don't worry! This chapter will give practical advice on how to do this and still enable you to maintain a work–life balance.

Teachers often feel the best way to plan for a pupil with learning difficulties is to look for workbooks or materials suitable for the pupil's academic ability level. The effect of this approach is that, even in Key Stage 2, the pupil ends up working through infant workbooks with a teaching assistant, and the work they undertake has no connection with the work of the rest of the class. In this scenario the pupil with SEN may rarely have any attention from the teacher, resulting in him/her being 'minded' rather than being taught.

Schools are bombarded constantly with advertisements for new and better materials for pupils with special needs. New sets of books or items of software promise to sort out the planning and meet pupil needs, but all too often they can add to the complexity. In fact, a teacher's brains and creativity are far superior to any new software or textbook. Try to ignore the blandishments of advertising. Totally different resources and activities are not necessary. The answers are rarely found in new resources, no matter how glossy the catalogue or impressive the claim. Talent and experience among teachers and teaching assistants are the most powerful factors in determining a pupil's potential for progress.

Targets and progress

No matter how excellent the teaching and care given, pupils with learning difficulties will fall behind their peers in academic development. The gap will become increasingly wide as the children move through the primary school. Because of this it is really important to track the pupil's progress carefully and to celebrate all achievement no matter how small the step. By setting individual, achievable and appropriate targets, everyone can feel satisfied. Parents know their  child is making progress, teachers know they are meeting the pupil's needs, and the pupil feels a sense of achievement and fulfilment. The goals may not be the same as for other children but they are no less valid. The old adage of 'measuring what we value, rather than valuing what we can measure' holds true in this case. If a school values and celebrates all pupil achievements, academic or otherwise, the whole community is lifted and energised.

Incorporating objectives from other agencies

Increasingly, agencies such as speech and language therapy or occupational therapy are working in close co-operation with mainstream schools. The system of taking pupils out of class for therapy is now commonly being replaced by therapists working with teachers and teaching assistants, and incorporating therapy objectives into IEP and curricular targets. Therapists assess the pupil and give training to the teacher or to a teaching assistant. They devise a programme to be carried out in school, and return at regular intervals to check on progress and adjust the programme.

Where there is a good and professional relationship between therapist and school, this consultation model is more effective than the isolated 20 minutes of therapy each week. It makes better use of the therapist's time, and develops valuable skills for teachers and teaching assistants that can be used with other children. Parents are often wary of this system, particularly where the pupil has therapy time specified on his/her Statement of Special Educational Needs. Good communication between therapist, school and parents is needed to help parents understand that their child is actually receiving better and more effective therapy. Invite parents in to talk to the therapist, teacher and TA together, and to observe the daily therapy programme in practice.

When planning to include a pupil with learning difficulties, liaise with the therapists and the SENCO to see if there are therapy objectives that might link in with particular topics or units of work. Physiotherapy targets could be addressed in PE and games, occupational therapy targets in food technology, and speech and language therapy targets in literacy and drama. This means that the impact of the therapy can be multiplied without the pupil being withdrawn from classes.

Tracking back to success in English and maths

For pupils with learning difficulties in mainstream classrooms tracking back is the most effective method of setting appropriate learning objectives in literacy and numeracy. This approach enables all pupils, no matter what their level of attainment, to learn in a class of their chronological peers. The principle of this approach is that children work on *individually-appropriate objectives within shared classroom activities*.

The starting point for including pupils with learning difficulties is the objective for the whole class from the National Primary Strategy Framework documents for literacy or numeracy. Once the class objective has been decided, then the teacher tracks back through the framework documents to an earlier year group to find a related objective for the pupil with learning difficulties.

Work through the tracking back process with a teaching assistant who knows the pupil well. This will ensure the objective is appropriate for the individual, and the collaboration will spark off ideas for activities and resources. This knowledge about individual pupils is very important in order to decide on appropriate teaching strategies and the questioning styles that will provide the child with the motivation to learn.

For pupils in Key Stage 2 it may be necessary to track back into Key Stage 1. Where a pupil is working below Year R level, track back into the P scales (QCA 2001a) (see Chapter 5) which lead into Level 1 of the National Curriculum. Aim to identify appropriate objectives that will challenge pupils, but which are pitched at a relevant and realistic level. This process ensures that pupils experience the full range of the English and maths curriculum while working on objectives appropriate to their individual needs.

Take into account the different ways that pupils learn, and use this information to influence your choice of teaching strategies. Next, write down other areas of the child's development or behaviour that you wish to improve upon or teach. These other areas might come from the child's IEP, or they may be issues in particular subjects. For instance:

- turn-taking in circle time;
- working independently in art;
- taking responsibility for collecting his/her own equipment in PE.

This information then gives the basis for the pupil's work for a lesson or series of lessons – academic, personal and social objectives.

During the planning process for each half term, tracking back means the teacher can plan shared activities for all pupils in the class, rather than design completely separate activities for pupils with learning difficulties. The concept of pupils working on individually appropriate objectives within a shared activity is a powerful and effective way to include pupils with a diverse range of learning needs. While tracking back is appropriate for pupils with learning difficulties, tracking forward may be more appropriate for more able pupils.

The important final step is to return to the age-appropriate year in the framework to prepare the context in which to set the objective. This last step is vital if pupils are to experience the challenge of a broadening curriculum as they move through the primary school and prepare for the transition to secondary education.

Once the objectives and activities for the lessons have been planned, a teaching assistant could support the process further by collecting any additional resources before each lesson, and by recording the pupil's responses to the planned activities. This recording then informs future planning.

A sample recording form (Figure 3.1) is included on the accompanying CD.

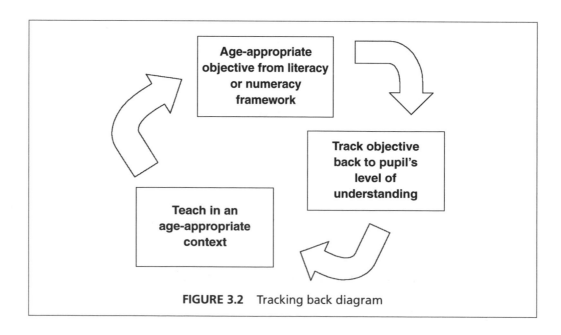

FIGURE 3.2 Tracking back diagram

Tracking back summarised:

1. Tracking back takes place at the medium-term planning stage.
2. Start from the age-appropriate objectives in the literacy or numeracy framework.
3. Track back through the literacy or numeracy primary framework, or into the P scales, to an objective appropriate and relevant to the needs of the pupil with learning difficulties.
4. Return to the age-appropriate year of the framework as this is the context in which the objective will be taught.
5. Identify class and group activities that address the objectives of all the class *and* the pupil with learning difficulties.

(See Figure 3.8b on CD: Tracking back grid: shape and space.)

The key concepts method

To ensure that lessons in other subjects are meaningful for all pupils in a class, a different approach needs to be taken. The *key concepts* method works particularly well in history, geography, PSHE and RE.

Once again the starting point is the class objectives. Before starting to plan for the term or half term for the subject, identify three or four facts or skills that you really want the pupil with learning difficulties to learn or develop – the key concepts of the lesson. For example, in history a Year 5 class learn 'How life has changed in the locality of the school since Victorian times'. The key concepts for a pupil with learning difficulties could be:

- Victoria was a queen of Great Britain
- the Victorians lived over one hundred years ago
- the railway came to our town in Victorian times.

In addressing these concepts the lesson will also develop specific skills in history, such as:

- to place events, people and changes into correct periods of time;
- to recall, select and organise historical information. (QCA 2000)

Planning for the class as a whole is then much easier. With the key concepts in mind, the teacher plans a variety of activities and resources that are accessible to the whole class *including* the child with learning difficulties. Additional resources and extension activities are built into the planning to cover learning of the key concepts, the class objectives and extension work for more able pupils. In this way children with learning difficulties are enabled to participate fully in the lesson, working in groups or with a partner. The sharp focus of two or three key concepts makes assessment much easier, and pupils learn more effectively when they know what is expected of them. As a part of what everyone else in the class is learning, the key concepts can be shared during the introduction to the lesson – written on the whiteboard or at the top of a worksheet – and referred to again in the plenary to check that they are understood.

In planning lessons to make key concepts accessible, ensure that the amount and the level of information matches the pupil's ability and understanding. Without this approach the sheer quantity of information in an undifferentiated

Name: Shelley   **Date:** 7.2.05   **Class/year group:** Y3   **Curriculum area:** Numeracy   **Teacher:** Miss Fisher   **T.A.:** Mr Cooper

	Support	Grouping	Resources	Recording	Key knowledge
Lesson starter	Meera and Mr Cooper	Pair with TA support	Number fans – to 10 for Shelley	Whiteboard shared	Recognise all coins (Y1 objective)
Main activity Task 1 Coin bingo	Mr Cooper and group	Small group with Meera, John and Peter	Coin bingo cards and real coins to £1	Photo of final card	Exchange coins up to 5p
Main activity Task 2 Shopping activity	Miss Fisher	Peter and Shelley with teacher	Ten items priced 1p to 5p. Coins in purse. Shopping basket	Worksheet	**Key vocabulary**
Plenary	Peter with Mr Cooper nearby	Pair with Peter	Coin fans – to 5p for Peter and Shelley	N/a	Money Coin Cost Buy Sell Pence Pound How much …? How many Total

FIGURE 3.3   Completed lesson differentiation planner

© Sue Briggs 2005

lesson, and the level of complexity of both the verbal and written language, will overwhelm pupils with learning difficulties. They cannot access such lessons at any level.

Key concepts in brief

Together the teacher and teaching assistant should:

- prepare the class objectives for the term or half term;
- look at the National Curriculum or P scales level description in the subject that matches the ability of the pupil with learning difficulties;
- identify two or three key concepts from the class objectives that match the level of understanding of the pupil;
- plan the lessons, incorporating group and individual activities that address the key concepts;
- prepare any additional resources;
- share the key concepts with the whole class;
- return to the key concepts at the end of the lesson to check understanding;
- assess against the key concepts after each lesson (and any IEP targets which may have been addressed).

Curriculum overlapping

A majority of pupils with learning difficulties need to spend additional school time working on IEP targets on communication, reading, writing and maths targets. In a mainstream primary school it is neither possible nor desirable regularly to withdraw pupils from class to work on these basic skills. An option allowing these skills to be developed without the withdrawal is curriculum overlapping.

In curriculum overlapping the pupil with learning difficulties joins in all lessons with his/her chronological age group. For some lessons, while the rest of the class work on subject objectives in, for example, history, geography or science, the pupil with learning difficulties focuses on literacy or numeracy targets from their IEP. In an ICT lesson a pupil may be working on developing mouse control, and additionally working on software to develop his/her understanding of number bonds. In this way the context for the learning is the subject area, but another IEP area is also being addressed. The pupil with learning difficulties will still be expected to work in groups of varying sizes, or with a partner, so careful planning is necessary for this approach to work.

Curriculum overlapping must be developed by the SENCO, teacher and any teaching assistants working together as a team. There needs to be careful planning to give the pupil opportunities to address the IEP targets while maintaining his/her entitlement to a broad and balanced curriculum.

> **CASE STUDY** **Kamal**
>
> Kamal is in Year 4 and he has Williams Syndrome. He has good expressive language but his comprehension is comparatively delayed. Kamal has a reading age of below six years. His IEP target for writing is:
>
> > Kamal will write two or three word captions to match pictures.
>
> In geography, Year 4 is working on how settlements develop.
> All the class, including Kamal, works with a partner. Each pair has a sheet of A3 paper with a river marked on it. Kamal and his partner have a key at the side of the paper and a number of small symbols of houses, a church, a school, a pond, a village green, etc. with which to create their own settlement. The class then share their settlements, and discuss how they differ. Kamal is confident in this situation, and with his partner talks animatedly about the village they have created. He then works with a teaching assistant at the computer to write three short sentences about the village using a laptop with Clicker 5 software.

Curriculum overlapping can also be used to address other IEP targets.

> **CASE STUDY** **Pippa**
>
> Pippa's IEP includes a behaviour target as she finds it very difficult to sit still and concentrate for more than five minutes at a time. In the same geography lesson as Kamal Pippa is working on the target 'I will stay in my seat and work for ten minutes'. Pippa's teacher has created a geography box for her that includes four ten-minute tasks, two for her to work on alone, and two to be completed with a partner. In her box for this lesson, Pippa has:
>
> - an A4 version of the blank village and pictures of buildings to stick on;
> - a 20-piece puzzle with a village scene;
> - a cut-up sentence about the village for her to read, match and reassemble;
> - a 'computer' symbol card that Pippa knows means she can use the computer, working on drag-and-drop software to create a village.
>
> In between the tasks Pippa is allowed to get up and walk around the classroom, go to the toilet or take a message to another member of staff.
> The context in which she is working is a Year 4 geography lesson but it is the IEP behaviour target that will be the focus of the lesson and the assessment for Pippa.

Richness of experience

The element that unites all these systems of planning for inclusion – tracking back, key concepts and curriculum overlapping – is experiential learning. By offering a curriculum enriched with relevant experiences the child with learning difficulties shares that richness with the other children in the class. Progress is about more than meeting IEP targets or assessment scores, important though they may be. Progress in terms of experiences and expectations is just as important and equally relevant. All the class will benefit when lessons are planned to include active, experiential and multi-sensory learning.

Learning styles

All children have their own areas of relative strength and weakness and all good teachers help children to develop individual areas of weakness whilst maximising strengths. Identification of the preferred learning style of individual children supports this good practice, and provides an additional perspective for curriculum and lesson planning.

There are three principle learning styles:

- visual
- auditory
- kinaesthetic.

Everyone learns by using a combination of all three styles, but individuals do have a preferred or dominant learning style. Children with special educational needs will have a dominant style which could be compromised by the child's particular learning difficulties. For example, visual learners relate most effectively to information in the form of writing or pictures, but a child with reading difficulties will have impaired access to written information and so would have to rely on auditory or kinaesthetic channels. Access to written information for this pupil could be facilitated through the use of symbols or by a talking word processor, so enabling the child to work to his or her relative strength.

It is useful for teachers to be aware of individual learning styles, but by planning opportunities for visual, auditory and kinaesthetic learning in every lesson, all pupils are given an equal opportunity to succeed.

Making connections

For pupils with learning difficulties the ability to generalise information and skills from one context to another is an area of particular weakness. Even where the children show understanding and attainment in one context, it cannot be assumed that they will be able to transfer and use that understanding and knowledge in a different context. For example, in the classroom a pupil may know and use all the coins to make amounts and give change, but may not be able to use those same money skills in a shop or on the bus.

Where possible find and build on links with other subjects to help pupils generalise information across subjects. Make those links explicit. Remind the pupil what they have learned previously, and show the relevant page in his/her book. In each lesson take a photograph of the pupil either holding an object related to the topic or involved in an activity. This will help the child to remember the lesson and to begin to make the necessary links to other areas of the curriculum.

As the curriculum in Key Stage 2 develops into more discrete subjects, the links between the different areas of the curriculum – say music and science – become less obvious. However, all pupils benefit when cross-curricular themes can be identified and the connections between subjects made explicit.

Concept maps are a valuable way of making visual links between subjects and information. A concept map is made up of words, colours, lines and/or pictures. The map helps pupils to organise their thinking and remember information. If the pupil is not able to do it for him or herself an adult can create the concept map. Using different colours, shapes, pictures and even photographs, the concept map supports learning and aids memory. Keep the maps clear and simple or they will only add further to the pupil's confusion. 'Kidspiration' and 'Inspiration' software (Inspiration Software Inc.) helps pupils who have reading and writing difficulties understand concepts by organising and categorising information visually.

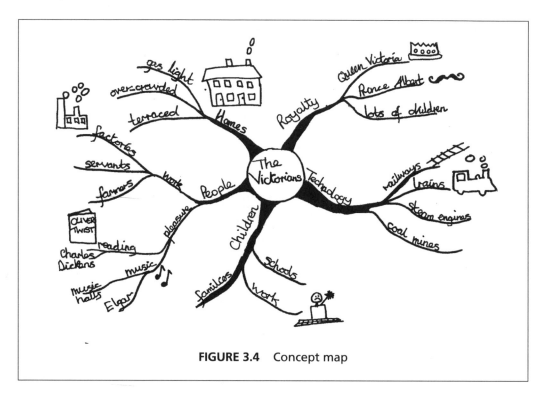

FIGURE 3.4   Concept map

Revisiting concepts

The first time around, pupils with learning difficulties will rarely learn and retain information. They will need opportunities to revisit and consolidate concepts several times and in different situations. The old army sergeant adage, 'Tell 'em what you're going to tell 'em; tell 'em; then tell 'em what you've just told 'em' describes just the right approach for pupils with learning difficulties – but not in the same tone of voice!

Make the objective clear at the start of the lesson so the pupils know what they are to be taught, and what they are expected to learn. Teach the concept through a variety of activities and with a range of resources. Then go back to the objective to show the pupil what they have learned.

Multi-sensory learning

The majority of lessons in primary schools are stimulating and lively, but pupils are still expected actively to listen, to the teacher or to each other, for sustained periods of time. Active listening is a skill that most children develop to a greater or lesser extent throughout the primary phase. This ability however will vary enormously in any class and must not be taken for granted. An over-emphasis on listening in lessons will impede the progress of a number of children:

- pupils who have a preferred visual or kinaesthetic learning style;
- any pupils with hearing loss or visual impairment;
- those with learning or communication difficulties.

This will encompass a significant group of pupils in every class, particularly in the winter months when something as minor as a cold can significantly reduce hearing acuity. A sensory impairment does not need to be severe to have a profound impact on learning – an out of date, or dirty, pair of prescription spectacles, for example, will limit a student's vision.

CASE STUDY   Meera

Meera has Down's Syndrome. She suffers from frequent bad colds throughout the winter causing her to have a significant hearing loss and difficulty with breathing. Meera had returned to school after the worst of her cold but her behaviour was unusually moody and she was reluctant to read or write. The reason for these changes was discovered when her teacher sat beside her and happened to look through Meera's glasses. Both lenses were covered in a layer of mucus, obscuring her vision. (Meera cannot blow her nose, so she wipes her hand from her nose up over her glasses, smearing the lenses in the process.) She returned to her usual sunny self once her glasses had been cleaned.

All pupils benefit from teaching styles which maximise multi-sensory involvement and promote active learning. In the foundation stage and Key Stage 1 the curriculum is founded on play-based learning, with practical activities giving children the opportunity to explore through all senses. They are encouraged to run, climb, stretch, roll and explore the world around them. As children progress through the primary phase however, the amount of exploration and practical activity gradually diminishes until it is largely limited to drama, PE, and design and technology lessons. Some pupils need more activity well into the later years of junior school, and it is unreasonable to expect these children to sit still for a protracted length of time. 'Brain Gym' type activities are valuable for breaking up lessons and refocusing pupils, and the simple exercises can enhance learning and build self-confidence (Cohen and Goldsmith 2000). The Brain Gym movements and games are also valuable for developing whole-class co-operation and collaboration.

By linking activities to tasks teachers will give children the opportunities for movement that they need and can enhance learning. For example, in the geography lesson above, if the teacher gave each group a large piece of paper on the floor on which to create their village maps, the children could get up and down from the floor, walk around, stretch and bend – and still stay on-task. It is useful to monitor pupils' activity in lessons across the school to identify where additional opportunities for movement can be built into planning. A checklist (Figure 3.5) for this purpose is included on the accompanying CD.

Variation and pace

Our pupils are used to receiving information from the media in short sharp bites – just watch any television programme aimed at older children and count the seconds between scene changes or new camera angles. Teachers should use this technique too, and devise varied activities that allow pupils to work in short bursts to make lessons interesting and memorable. But the rapid pace of some lessons does serve to exclude certain pupils: those children with learning difficulties, those with communication difficulties, those with attention disorders, and those with sensory impairments. It is important for lessons to have pace, but the same pace does not need to be maintained throughout. Vary the pace, and break up the lesson into shorter activities, and you will help all pupils and the better include those with any learning challenges.

The planning for this type of lesson fits in well with the Primary Strategy that recommends a three part lesson: a whole class session, group work and then a plenary.

Whole class starter

If this initial session is planned to be fast-paced, then support pupils with learning difficulties with response cards, number or letter fans, or whiteboards. Sit each child with a partner and ask them to discuss the question before answering.

Whole class focused teaching

This part of the lesson can be taken at a more considered pace. Once again, the arrangement of children in pairs or small groups means that the learning of all children can be supported. Judicious deployment of teaching assistants and resources will offer differentiated support to those children experiencing barriers to learning.

Independent and group work

All children should be given tasks that they can complete confidently without the need for adult intervention. Where the planned task matches the child's level of ability and understanding, any pupil should be expected to work independently, or co-operatively within a group. A sand timer will help the pupil gauge how long they have to complete the task and a simple work schedule using pictures or symbols will tell him/her what to do next.

Plenary

Plenary sessions are invaluable for all pupils, both as the opportunity to revisit the lesson objective and evaluate what the class as a whole has learned, and to move learning on in preparation for the next lesson. Make sure that all the children in the class have the chance to share their work, with adults responding positively to children's comments and acknowledging the effort behind the child's work.

'Mini-plenaries' are useful to refocus the class midway through independent and group work. They serve to draw together what the children have already done, and the task can then be consolidated or adapted according to individual need.

Practical experiences and apparatus

When planning to include pupils with learning difficulties, identify every possible opportunity for them to use practical hands-on equipment and to engage in first-hand experiences; abstract concepts will not be understood unless they are linked to real-life concrete examples and experiences. They might hear about the Victorians in history, but they need the chance to see and go into Victorian houses, hold artefacts from the period and wear Victorian clothes. In a maths class working on fractions, give the pupil with learning difficulties a piece of card to cut into halves, quarters and eighths. Teachers sometimes find that practical activities such as this throw up challenging questions. In a lesson on 2D shape, a pupil would not accept the plastic shapes that were offered. She insisted the shapes were 3D because she could see the 1 mm edges. How thin does a 3D shape have to be to become 2D? Not the kind of philosophical question one would expect from a pupil with learning difficulties, but these children often bring fresh perspectives that challenge assumptions.

Health and safety

Safety issues related to a child with learning difficulties, or the safety of other children, need to be resolved when planning an inclusive curriculum. Obvious areas of concern are in design and technology lessons where some children may be unaware of the potential dangers of equipment such as hand saws or hot glue guns. Risk assessments are necessary for these activities, but planning these activities with the child with learning difficulties at the forefront of your thinking resolves many of the issues at the outset.

For example, in design and technology, corrugated plastic that can be cut with scissors is an alternative to wood, and low-melt glue guns are available which avoid the blisters. Wall bars are often cited as reason for withdrawing pupils with learning difficulties from PE lessons, but there are other, less potentially dangerous pieces of equipment that give children the chance to use the same range of movements and muscle groups, such as agility tables with low level bridging and linking apparatus.

Other sensory cues

The sense of smell is not only linked to taste, it also has powerful links to memory and emotions. Think of a juicy orange, the Christmas turkey roasting in the oven, a freshly-mown lawn. Can you smell them right now?

It is possible to use the senses of smell and taste to increase concentration and aid memory. Try having indigenous foods in the classroom when learning about a new country in geography, incense or myrrh in an RE session about Christian faiths, or a pomander when learning about the Elizabethans in history. A scented candle burning in the room will help pupils focus and remember the lesson when they are trying to recall information at a later date. Chapter 4 gives more detail about additional visual and sensory supports for learning.

Verbal delivery

Have you listened to yourself when you are teaching? Very few teachers have recorded their lessons, and really listened to how they sound from a pupil's perspective. It is a fascinating exercise and very worthwhile. Teachers are good communicators. They have a lot to say and they say it well. But they say it fast! Teachers also move around and do other things as they speak; they turn to face the whiteboard, give out books or write a note. A slower verbal delivery helps both the teacher and the pupils. It gives the teacher time to think and choose words more carefully. It means pupils understand more of what is being said. Look at the class when you are addressing them so they can see your face, and use eye contact and gesture to enhance the meaning of what you say.

One question at a time

The use of questions is an integral part of teaching. Teachers ask questions to check understanding and knowledge, to develop pupils' thinking, and to make lessons more interactive. Teachers often ask a question and then immediately ask it again, rephrased to aid understanding, and there will be some pupils who will have formulated the answer and have their hand up even before the teacher has finished asking the initial question. Pupils with learning difficulties need time both to hear and to process a question, search for the information they need for the answer, formulate a response, and then answer. This will take longer than you think. A slow count of ten is a useful length of time to allow for a considered response. If, while they are still thinking, the teacher rephrases the question and asks it again, the pupil with learning difficulties will need to start the whole process again. In effect, they are being asked a new question before having had the chance to answer the previous one. This scenario makes pupils with learning difficulties confused and sometimes distressed, and can frequently lead to challenging behaviour.

One way to avoid this situation is to prepare the pupil with learning difficulties for the questions in advance. The pupil could work on them at home with parents, or in a one-to-one session with a teaching assistant, so that he/she will be prepared when the questions are asked in class. Alternatively, the pupil could work with a TA in the lesson to be ready to respond to a question in the plenary.

Make a note to yourself to ask a child with learning difficulties at least one question each lesson – and make sure it is a question they can answer. It can be soul-destroying for some children to sit through lesson after lesson, never having the chance or being able to answer a question correctly. Watch a child's self-esteem soar when they can show what they know.

Use of language

Using simplified language does not mean that teachers need to 'talk down' to pupils with learning difficulties. Problems often arise because teachers are such good communicators with wide vocabularies. When a pupil with learning difficulties is in the class, try to say what you mean. English is ambiguous, full of inference, homonyms and synonyms. Be aware that a pupil is likely to misunderstand spoken information if they do not have additional cues, such as objects, pictures or signs.

CASE STUDY   **Louis**

Louis is in Year 1. He has Autistic Spectrum Disorder. Since starting at the school he has consistently refused to go into the hall for PE. He is reluctant to come to school on PE days and is upset throughout that day. His parents and teacher assume he does not like going into the large hall, even though he happily joins in assembly every morning. A volunteer offered to stay in class with Louis during a PE lesson. The volunteer asked him why he didn't like PE. He answered, 'It's rude' and the volunteer mentioned this to the teacher who realised that Louis had mistaken the term PE for 'pee' – he thought the children were going to the toilet together in the hall. His teacher changed the name of PE to games and the next week Louis happily joined in the lesson.

Subject or topic specific vocabulary

Words that have more than one meaning can cause comprehension problems. For example, the word 'difference' may mean 'unlikeness' in common usage, but when asked to find the difference between two numbers, pupils need to know that in the context of a numeracy lesson it means subtraction of the smaller number from the larger. If you ask a child with learning difficulties to draw a table in maths, do not be surprised if what you get is what you sit at to eat your tea! A way around this is to give pupils a simple glossary book in which they write down new words with the meaning of the word in the particular context. This sort of work can be valuable preparation for starting new topics and can be planned by the teaching assistant and/or given as homework. It can be a huge boost to self-esteem if at the beginning of a lesson a pupil with learning difficulties can explain to the class the definition of a newly introduced word.

Choices

Everyone needs to be able to make sensible choices if they are to lead independent lives in adulthood. The reality for most pupils with learning difficulties is that just about everything they do is directed by adults. Sadly, it is not uncommon to see pupils in Year 6 having their books opened for them and being handed a pen by a teaching assistant. It is interesting to have a member of staff monitor a pupil with learning difficulties over one or two days, to log how many opportunities the pupil has to make choices. If children are deprived of choice they will give up trying to think for themselves and become over-reliant on adults for all their needs. As the child moves through the school, build increasing opportunities for choice into lessons, choices as basic as which pen or pencil to use, who to work with or where to sit. All will the better prepare the child for transfer to secondary school.

Individual subject targets

Short-term subject targets that are understood by and agreed with the pupil with learning difficulties will provide an effective means of measuring progress over time. Targets may be linked to the pupil's Individual Education Plan or may refer to skills and information specific to a subject. Make the targets visible by sticking them in the front of the exercise book and refer to them at the start and end of every lesson. A target needs to be worded in such a way that, when it is achieved, the pupil is able to say, 'Yes, I can do that.' For example, a science target such as, 'Samir will recognise and name common types of material: wood, metal, plastic, paper and rock' is easy to record and assess. Samir understands what she has to learn and she and her parents will know when she has achieved her target.

Recording

Thankfully, the days are long past when pupils spent much time copying down writing from the blackboard, although most recording in schools is still in hand-writing, as are most of the ways that pupils show attainment. Nowadays there are numerous alternatives to written methods that make recording more accessible and often more fun. Pupils making a video or audio diary can show greater understanding than in a written essay. Drawings or photo-montages often reveal great insight. Software packages, such as Clicker 5, give on-screen word banks and pictures that make writing less slow and arduous. Alternatives to writing can produce startling results – both for children with learning difficulties and those without.

Children with all kinds of learning challenges will face problems with note-taking or recording information in class. For many the problem will be the spelling or the required speed of writing. In literacy lessons it may be necessary to focus on written tasks, but in other subjects teachers need to ask themselves why the pupils need to write; what is the purpose of the writing? For example, is it necessary for a child to write in a history lesson for him/her to learn and remember the information? The use of pictures, photographs, audio tape or video would serve as well, if not better, than half a page of handwriting. As long as the key information is recorded in some form, the format is not important.

By accepting a range of methods of recording teachers will be liberating pupils with learning difficulties from the tyranny of the pen. Some pupils with learning difficulties may think of a wonderful sentence but will have forgotten it by the time they have finished writing the first word. This does not mean that teachers should give up on developing pupils' writing ability, but there is little point in their simply copying an adult's writing which they do not understand and cannot read back. Here are some ideas for alternative ways of recording.

Photographs

A cheap digital camera will revolutionise recording for pupils with learning difficulties. Photograph pupils as they take part in practical activities or allow them to sequence a series of photographs of, for example, a science activity or experiment.

Computers

Laptop or desktop computers with symbol software or Clicker 5 grids give pupils with learning difficulties an independent way of recording what they have learned. Clicker 5 grids for a wide range of subjects at Key Stages 1 and 2 are available on the internet at www.LearningGrids.com. Most of the grids have been designed by teachers who have put them on the website for others to use.

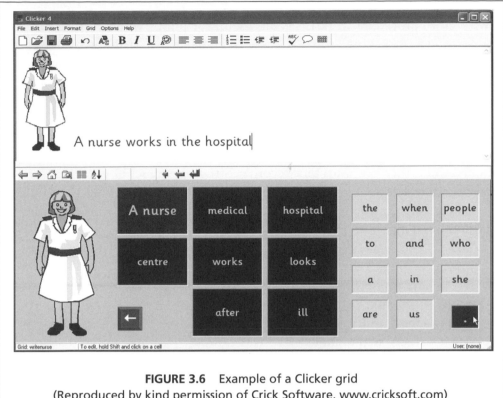

FIGURE 3.6   Example of a Clicker grid
(Reproduced by kind permission of Crick Software, www.cricksoft.com)

Drawings

Some pupils with learning difficulties are able to draw a picture based on what they have learned. They need to be able to look at the pictures on a future date and understand the meaning behind them. Ask the pupil to tell an adult about the picture, and then scribe exactly what is said. This will inform a teacher's assessment of how much the pupil has understood and learned.

Video and audio recordings

Recording lessons on audio tapes (or on video if you are feeling brave) means that pupils can watch or listen to the lesson several times over, either in school or at home. Allow pupils to record their own interpretation of the key lesson objectives on audio or video tape, and this will quickly build up into a bank of resources that can be used both for recording and for assessment. If pupils are taught to speak each sentence into a Dictaphone as they write, and then rewind and listen, they can be freed from the need for constant one-to-one support.

Sequencing

Worksheets are a valuable way of offering appropriately differentiated work for pupils of different abilities, and where the worksheets are well designed most pupils enjoy working through them. A useful way of using worksheets to develop skills for pupils with learning difficulties is to design the worksheets as a cut and stick sequencing activity. Mix up pictures and corresponding sentences on the worksheet. The pupil cuts them out and sequences the pictures in the right order and then matches the sentences. No matter what the subject this approach works well. The pupil does not need to write, and the activity involves fine motor skills, reading, and if organised as a paired or group activity, speaking and listening.

Cloze procedure

Simple cloze procedure worksheets are useful for pupils who can read but who find writing and spelling difficult. These worksheets can easily be differentiated with the missing words and symbol supports at the bottom or at the side of the page.

Scribing

Scribing is a valuable technique to use when teachers want a pupil's ideas and creativity really to shine through. Pupils can speak either directly to another pupil or an adult, or they can use a tape recorder. Structure the scribing with questions, pictures or objects, and avoid the pupil losing the thread of what they want to say. When teaching poetry, give each of the pupils an object to hold – a piece of fruit perhaps. One child has an orange:

- Look at it – bright, orange, round;
- feel it – smooth, soft;
- peel it – furry, wet;
- smell it – fresh, fruity, tangy;
- taste it – sharp, sweet, juicy.

Write down the words they use and you have the basis of a poem. Each child will respond in different ways, with different understanding and using different language. Inclusive activities of this kind allow all children to achieve and to share that achievement as equals.

Photographs

Flashcards

On-screen word banks (Clicker 5, Writing with Symbols 2000)

Drawings/pictures

Symbols

Audio tape

Video tape

PowerPoint presentation

Sequencing pictures and/or text

Cut and stick worksheets

Cloze procedure

Scribing

FIGURE 3.7 Alternatives to writing for recording and presenting information

Assessment

Measure what you value rather than value what you can measure. Repeating this saying is not a mistake. For pupils with learning difficulties it is a necessity. For some pupils, one step up from P8 to Level 1 of the National Curriculum is just as important an achievement as is gaining Level 5 in Key Stage 2 tests for their peers. This book recommends setting for pupils with learning difficulties a few precise targets across the curriculum. IEP targets can be used to show progress in core skills, but for foundation subjects, if children are learning science or geography, teachers need to know how effective their teaching has been, and what the child has learned. These precise targets are easier to assess and having only two or three targets limits the paperwork.

Where targets are based on P scales or National Curriculum level descriptors, pupils can be assessed against national benchmarks. This gives schools the information they need to show the value added for a particular pupil. It is useful to instigate across the curriculum a system of observations of a pupil with learning difficulties which identify successful strategies and which gain impartial insights into pupil behaviour. The observations feed into the assessment process, and so into planning for future inclusion. A form for recording these observations (Figure 3.8) can be found on the accompanying CD.

For pupils with learning difficulties an effective way of recording achievement is the keeping of an 'experience folder'. Each folder should encompass one academic year and can include pieces of work, computer print outs, paintings, drawings, photographs and souvenirs of visits or special occasions, such as the programme for the school production. Assessments, school reports and completed IEPs can be kept in a separate file or as part of the main folder. Over time these folders will build up a valuable record of the pupil's achievements and experiences and provide evidence of progress and attainment.

SATs and other tests

There is no point in a child sitting tests in areas in which they cannot achieve. Testing at the end of Key Stage 1 should pose no problems, as teachers now have more control over which tasks or tests children undertake. Teachers have the flexibility to choose the best time for the tests to be taken appropriate for the level at which the child is working.

The assessment arrangements for Key Stage 2, however, do remain a potential barrier to participation for pupils with learning difficulties. Not only are the tests themselves inappropriate for children working at earlier levels of the National Curriculum, but the period of time leading up to the tests involves revision and specific preparation for the tests.

The most effective and inclusive way of managing this time is to give the child with learning difficulties equivalent work and experiences. This exam situation is a recurring feature of the life experience of other children and young people, and can be shared by children with learning difficulties, preferably without the anxiety. The study skills necessary for Key Stage 2 assessment are equally beneficial for all pupils about to transfer to secondary school. Prepare work that is linked to the theme of the assessment work which the child can complete independently.

If at all possible during the exam period allow the pupil with learning difficulties to work alongside classmates on an individual project that can be used as part of their own assessment profile. The SATs week is a stressful and difficult time for all children and staff, and the resulting challenges to inclusion could spoil a child's final weeks in the school.

Summary

What makes inclusion successful in the primary school?

- **Planning**: Tracking back, key concepts or curriculum overlapping make it possible to plan to include a pupil with learning difficulties as part of the planning for the rest of the class.
- **Teamwork**: With parents, the child, teachers, colleagues, the SENCO, teaching assistants and other professionals.
- **Flexibility**: Accept different ways of recording and different ways of communicating.
- **Links**: Make links between subjects explicit and visual.
- **Supports**: Look beyond teaching assistants to peer support, visual and other sensory supports and information technology.
- **Assessment**: Measure what you value.

Chapter 4 looks at support for inclusion in more detail.

Support for inclusion

What is learning support?

The Index for Inclusion (Booth *et al.* 2000) defines learning support as 'all activities which increase the capacity of a school to respond to student diversity'. The authors of the Index clearly see learning support as a whole-school issue, aimed at supporting the development of more inclusive systems in the school rather than merely helping individual children. If support is to be wholly effective it must be founded on respect for the pupil with learning difficulties, and that pupil's right to be a part of the school community.

Learning support comes in many different forms, shapes and sizes, and to be most effective needs to permeate all areas of school life.

Support for learning will come from:

- teaching assistants and other adults
- other pupils
- teaching styles
- visual and other sensory supports
- information technology
- resources
- outside agencies.

Support that is clearly defined, structured and consistent makes the difference between a successful long-term placement and one that ends in failure.

Among both teachers and support staff there are often fundamental misunderstandings about inclusion, and what inclusion really means.

People ask,

'How can it be inclusion if one child gets much more than another?'

or

'There are lots of pupils who would attain much more if they had a teaching assistant.'

or

'It isn't fair that pupils with learning difficulties have teaching assistants while others don't.'

or

'Inclusion means all children doing the same thing.'

All who are involved with pupils who have learning difficulties need to be familiar with the school's inclusive ethos, and to subscribe to both policy and practice. Appropriate training will help to shape attitudes and ensure that everyone is 'singing from the same hymn sheet'. The training activities below are a useful way to start discussion and develop understanding about inclusion. They are suitable for use with school staff, governors and parents.

TRAINING ACTIVITY 1   **Inclusion – definitions**

Organisation: whole group together with one person recording what is said on a flipchart.

Resources:
- paper and pens
- box
- flipchart.

1. Each person writes a brief definition of inclusion.
2. The definitions are folded and placed in a box.
3. The box is shaken and everyone takes out a definition.
4. This definition is shared with one other person and key words noted, e.g. all, welcome, etc.
5. Write the key words on a flipchart.
6. As a group, use the key words to write a definition of inclusion with which all can agree.

TRAINING ACTIVITY 2   **The 'no buts' zone**

Organisation: all together, seated in a circle.

Resources: one red chair – the 'hot seat'.

The group moves around the circle, from one chair to the next. The person sitting in the 'hot seat' says something positive about including pupils who have learning difficulties, or they move on to the next chair without comment. A previously used comment may be repeated. The only rule is that no-one is allowed to say 'but'.

This is a very simple yet powerful activity. Hearing the positive benefits of inclusion without the negatives – the 'buts' – begins to change perceptions and attitudes.

TRAINING ACTIVITY 3	On the cards

Organisation: groups of four people.

Resources:
- One envelope for each group
- Each envelope contains one card with the integration definition below, one card with the inclusion definition, and two blank cards.

Integration
A process by which individual children are supported in order that they can participate in the existing (and largely unchanged) programme of the school.

Inclusion
A willingness to restructure the school's programme in response to the diversity of the pupils who attend.

FIGURE 4.1 Activity definition cards

1. In the groups, open the envelope and set out the cards with the integration card on the left, the inclusion card on the right, and the two blank cards in between.
2. Discuss the definitions.
3. On each of the blank cards, write down an action a school could take to move from the integration model to inclusion as defined on the cards.
4. As a plenary, write up all actions on a flipchart and discuss with the whole group.

Inclusion does not mean that everyone should receive the same provision, nor does it mean that all children should fit into the same systems in school. It is up to schools to adapt systems to meet the needs of a more diverse group of pupils, and to ensure that every pupil receives the provision that s/he needs. In *inclusive* schools each child is given the level of provision and support they needed, and receives it regardless of ability.

For children with learning difficulties in mainstream schools all too often the reality is that they spend every lesson sitting next to an adult, and speaking mostly to adults. It is sad to see a pupil with learning difficulties working hard for every minute of the lesson with an adult making sure he/she stays on task. Look around the class – you will see other children chatting quietly, gazing out of the window or just daydreaming. Very few pupils work consistently throughout lessons, yet often this is what is expected of pupils with learning difficulties. They probably work harder than the majority of their classmates.

Teaching assistants and other adults

The growth in the number of teaching assistants in schools has been a very positive development in recent years. Support given to groups or individual pupils by TAs can improve access to the curriculum, raise self-esteem, encourage positive behaviour, and have a beneficial effect on the whole of the class.

In both medium-term and lesson planning it is important that teaching assistants are involved so that they understand the aims of the lessons, and are aware of the teacher's expectations of their role in that context. This is equally necessary for teaching assistants assigned to a class as for those whose identified role is to support an individual child with learning difficulties.

The ideal situation is for the child who has learning difficulties to develop good working relationships with all the adults in the classroom, including parent helpers. This can be achieved by scheduling all adults to support the pupil over the course of a week. This variety of support will also give different perspectives on the child's progress and attainment that will inform assessments, target setting and reports.

Teaching assistants should always be deployed in ways that foster the independence of pupils, which enable them to be full and valued members of the class. In effect the most successful teaching assistants are working themselves out of a job! The day when a child no longer needs individual TA support ought to be a day of celebration.

Individual support

The majority of pupils with more severe learning difficulties will have a number of support hours allocated through their Statements of Special Educational Needs, or through the special educational needs funding system of the LEA. These hours often cover most of the time the pupil is in school. The close relationship that develops between a pupil with learning difficulties and the teaching assistant supporting them can be very positive. Equally, the situation can become oppressive for both parties when they are expected to work together for long periods of time.

Where a pupil has additional behavioural difficulties, the teaching assistant is often the only person who knows the pupil well enough to encourage him/her to stay on task, and too often is the only person dealing directly with the inappropriate behaviours. This situation causes intolerable stress and cannot be maintained in the long term.

Where a pupil has a high number of teaching assistant hours it is always best to share those hours between at least two TAs, so that if one person is ill another can provide cover. It also helps to prevent the pupil from becoming dependent on one particular teaching assistant. Ideas, strategies and tasks can also be shared during 'overlap' periods when both adults are in school.

Support hours detailed on statements need not tie one particular teaching assistant to a pupil for the amount of time specified. Schools are free to deploy teaching assistants to the best advantage of the pupils in a particular situation. Try adjusting working times for one or two days each week, so that teaching assistants arrive before the start of school or stay after the end of the school day. These measures create opportunities for TAs to:

- talk to other teaching assistants;
- differentiate lessons with teachers;
- prepare resources;
- share training;
- attend staff meetings;
- contribute to annual review reports.

All these activities provide support just as much as having the teaching assistant seated next to the pupil. Involving teaching assistants in planning, and ensuring they have plenty of positive feedback about their work, gives them the professional status they deserve.

Support for independence
- knowing when to stand back and encourage pupil to make own decisions
- expecting pupil to work unsupported for part of each lesson
- developing independence in physical needs, such as using the toilet

Social interaction
- supporting pupil as member of a collaborative group
- promoting peer acceptance and understanding
- helping pupil develop social and organisational skills
- organising games to include the child with learning difficulties

Professional liaison
- working alongside teachers to plan curriculum access and set targets
- delivering programmes devised to meet specific needs
- observing and recording pupil responses
- monitoring behaviour, e.g. time spent on task
- releasing the teacher so s/he can work with small groups
- liaising with other professionals
- contributing to annual and transition reviews
- preparing appropriate resources

FIGURE 4.2   What support might look like

Support at playtime and dinner time

Some children have support hours detailed for the unstructured time in school, such as dinner or playtime. Where a TA supports a pupil at break times, avoid the TA taking on the role of 'minder'. The most effective role at playtime is that of distant observer: close enough to intervene if necessary, but at a distance that allows the child to interact independently with others. This is a valuable opportunity for formal and informal observations of a pupil's social skills, and for identifying areas for development. Alternatively, organise group games and activities that all children can play and enjoy; games like 'What's the time, Mr Wolf', Ring a Ring of Roses . . . even the Hokey Cokey!

Where a child is supported by a lunchtime supervisor for dinner play it is imperative that training is available *before* the supervisor starts to support the pupil. This is not a situation where a willing mum can be drafted in at short notice. There must also be daily communication with the class teacher and teaching assistants so that the supervisor is aware of all important information regarding the child; such as, for example, any changes in behaviour strategies.

Support towards independence

All children need to develop individual and group working skills as they grow if they are to become more independent. Stand back and allow pupils to make their own decisions – this is a vital part of one-to-one support. Even when support is needed for toileting, pupils should be encouraged to be responsible for as much of their own care as possible. It is very difficult to wean off individual support once pupils have become dependent, so they need to get used to working without support for part of every lesson, if at first for only five minutes. For this to be possible, teachers will need to devise activities that can be completed without constant support. Simple activities such as insert puzzles, matching peg board patterns, listening to a taped story, sorting games etc. are easy to prepare and have a definite finish. Releasing teaching assistants from the support of one pupil all the time also frees them to work with other pupils and gives more variety to their work.

Social interaction

Wherever possible, encourage pupils to work as part of a collaborative group, even if he/she already has one-to-one support. Social interaction is enhanced when pupils work together, for instance in a Jigsaw activity. Other pupils are often unsure how to speak to and behave with a pupil with learning difficulties, and a teaching assistant can be a valuable role model for positive and equal inter-actions.

Personal organisation

Children with learning difficulties often find it very difficult to organise their belongings. Visual reminders around the classroom will develop confidence for individual pupils, and foster better organisation for all the class. Hang on the door a notice board with pictures of the equipment needed for the next day. This reminds all the class as they leave at the end of the afternoon. Give a pupil a picture list of the equipment needed for a particular activity or lesson, e.g. swimming or PE kit. With these strategies pupils with learning difficulties gradually develop that sense of responsibility they will need when they transfer to secondary school.

Professional liaison

Teaching assistants who support pupils on a one-to-one basis need to have time to talk to the class teacher other than in lessons. This liaison must be timetabled, and given a high priority by leadership teams if it is not to be undermined by other imperatives. By discussing the pupil's progress together the teacher and TA can ensure access for the individual pupil and incorporate IEP objectives into lessons. Without this liaison teaching assistants have to work in isolation, and may need to adapt activities and resources that are inappropriate while a lesson is actually taking place.

Often teaching assistants will notice incidents in classrooms missed by teachers because of their necessary focus on the whole class – but may have no time to pass this information on at the end of the lesson. A concise form is a useful way of transferring information that can be used as part of the assessment process and which will inform the planning of future lessons.

Comments written by teaching assistants should be predominantly positive. Try to start out by writing what the pupil has done well, and then comment on areas of difficulty. For example:

> **CASE STUDY** **Karim**
>
> Extract from Karim's maths liaison form:
>
> **Year 5 Maths: Shape and Space: 3D shapes**
>
> Karim sat quietly and listened to the first part of the lesson. He tried hard in the group activity and named correctly the cube and cuboid. Karim had difficulty understanding the individual task. He became distressed and refused to attempt the work. When calm, he worked on a construction kit from his maths activity box and created several 3D shapes. Digital photographs were taken of finished shapes for Karim's maths folder.

This balanced and accurate information gives the teacher a firm basis for assessing Karim's level of understanding and informs future lesson planning, but it does not duck the issue of Karim's inappropriate behaviour. It puts into context a task he did not understand, and shows how the difficulties were resolved.

A form that can be used by teaching assistants to record pupil responses (Figure 4.3) is included on the accompanying CD.

Multi-disciplinary teams

Teaching assistants are a vital part of the multi-disciplinary team involved with a pupil, and close liaison with other professionals and parents will be necessary. This is especially the case if the TA is to work with the pupil on, for example, a fine motor skills programme under the direction of an occupational therapist. Where therapy targets or targets based on advice from other outside professionals are included in a pupil's IEP, there is a much more 'holistic' approach to meeting the child's needs. If these targets can then be incorporated as far as possible into planning for classroom activities, the need for withdrawal from class can be minimised. Remember, by withdrawing a child for therapy he/she misses some part of the curriculum in class. Achieving a balance between therapy and curricular imperatives can be difficult, and will depend on the individual needs of the child. Discussing this balance with therapists often leads to a creative solution and a plan for an effective series of lessons.

> **CASE STUDY** **Faith**
>
> Faith is in Year 2. She has difficulties with fine and gross motor skills and the occupational therapist has given the school a programme to follow. Faith worked on her programme for ten minutes during assembly each morning. At first, she seemed happy to be withdrawn, but over the next three weeks became less keen to leave the class, and said she wanted to go into assembly with everyone else. Her teacher realised that Faith's birthday was approaching and that Faith didn't want to miss her birthday song in assembly. The teacher and TA talked to the occupational therapist about the situation and he suggested that the whole class could do the exercises every day after dinner.

Many schools find that skills developed by teaching assistants can be used to support other children in the school. An example of how the inclusion of children with learning difficulties can be beneficial for all children in the school would be where a TA worked with a speech and language therapist on a speech and language programme for a pupil with learning difficulties. The skills learned by the TA enabled her the better to support other children in the school who had less complex speech or language difficulties.

Other adults

Other adults in school – parents and grandparents, volunteers, student teachers, governors – are a really valuable resource and an ideal way of varying the support for pupils who have learning difficulties. These involvements help the children develop social and interaction skills with a wider range of people. These new people bring fresh perspectives and expectations, even new topics of conversation, to expand a pupil's vocabulary.

Wider contacts with other adults also serve to reassure other parents about what they may think are the effects of the child with learning difficulties learning alongside their own children. Inclusion is a recent concept, and parents may be anxious, for instance, that the teacher might spend too long with the child with special educational needs at the expense of the rest of the class. The more people know about how an inclusive classroom works, and so appreciate the benefits for all children, the better.

Peer support

Peer support for pupils with learning difficulties is an effective and powerful tool for inclusion, yet schools often are remarkably reluctant to make use of a natural resource. There is a frequent fear that parents of the supporting pupils will object, that it is unfair on the other students, or that work will suffer as a consequence. Peer support in practice is rarely a burden for pupils, and is usually of benefit to all concerned. Buddy systems and Circles of Friends are powerful ways to include children who need a little help to become part of the school community.

Buddies

It is reasonable to expect one pupil to help another from time to time. A buddy system simply makes that help more formal and gives the supporters a framework within which to operate. The majority of buddy systems are based on pairing children in order to, for example, guide and support a new pupil through the initial settling-in process. Such a paired system could put too much responsibility on one child and so a buddy scheme involving a small number of supporters – four or five – is more appropriate for pupils who have learning difficulties.

Careful selection of buddies at the outset is important for the future success of the scheme. Buddies can be chosen either from the pupil's own class or from an older year group, depending on whether the support is for all the time in school, or only for breaks and lunchtimes. If the support is to be effective, preparation for the buddies is very important, with the boundaries of their role carefully defined. For example, the buddy's role in the playground might be to talk with the pupil with learning difficulties and encourage him/her to join games. The buddy would not be expected to intervene in disputes with other pupils, except to inform a member of staff. The amount of time spent in support should be limited, and buddies need to have time to give feedback to staff. There also needs to be time to discuss any issues that may arise. A written schedule of regular support and feedback meetings will protect all the parties from becoming overburdened.

CASE STUDY	Peter's buddy scheme

Peter is in Year 3 and four boys have volunteered to be in his buddy scheme. Peter's buddy sheet (Fig 4.4) shows how his four buddies take turns to play with him at play or dinner time. The system is planned to allow each boy sufficient opportunity to maintain his own friendship group. The buddy timetable is changed every week, and at the end of each month buddies are given the opportunity to drop out. Peter joins dance club on Tuesday evenings and Reshma volunteered to be his buddy in the club for the autumn term.

Mr Jones is Peter's teacher, and organised the buddy system with advice from the educational psychology service. He monitors the scheme closely and offers advice and support where necessary. He also arranges a weekly, informal meeting with squash and biscuits for all the buddies. The buddies are encouraged to discuss any problems that may have come up, and how they dealt with the situations. Each term Mr Jones arranges a 'treat' for the buddies, such as a group visit to the bowling alley or the swimming pool, and Peter is usually invited to join in the fun.

Talk partners

The talk partner system is used in many primary schools and is a valuable way of supporting less confident children. Talk partners support pupils with learning difficulties very well, enable them to answer questions and encourage speaking and listening.

Rather than pupils always putting up hands and answering questions verbally after talking in pairs, they could instead write or draw their answer and hold it up on a small whiteboard. This gives all pupils an opportunity to be involved in the activity. Sometimes teaching assistants act as a talk partner for the pupil they support, but it is more effective if the pupil has another child acting as the partner, with the TA supporting them both.

Circle of friends

The circles of friends approach originated in North America and has been used in mainstream settings to support children with a wide range of disabilities. The circle consists of between six and eight pupils who volunteer to form a support network for a particular child. The circle is led by an adult, usually an educational psychologist or a teacher. A weekly meeting with the whole circle is held to discuss any difficulties and to work out ways of resolving problems for the pupil.

The circles of friends has three main aims:

- to create for the child a support network of other pupils;
- to provide the child with encouragement and recognition for achievements and progress;
- to work with the child to identify difficulties and to come up with practical ideas to help sort out problems.

Setting up a circle includes:

- gaining the support and agreement of the focus pupil and his/her parents;
- a meeting with the whole class (which the focus pupil does not attend) aimed at identifying those willing to be supporters;
- informing the parents of those chosen to be circle members and gaining their agreement to their child's participation;
- weekly meetings of the circle, the focus pupil and an adult facilitator. (Newton and Wilson 1999)

The time commitment of the circle members needs to be monitored carefully to make sure the support is not taking up too much of their time, and is being shared equally amongst the group. The time commitment for staff is roughly 40 to 60 minutes to set up the circle, with weekly meetings each lasting 20 to 30 minutes. A bonus of the circles of friends approach is that where some of the circle members have behavioural, emotional or social difficulties, the circle often has a positive affect on their behaviour and self-esteem in school in addition to the positive support for the focus child.

Medication

An issue that causes schools much anxiety when planning to include pupils with learning difficulties is the administration of medicines. Medication may need to be administered regularly (an inhaler for asthma) or perhaps only in an emergency situation (following an epileptic seizure). Many pupils at some time need to take medicines in school, whether antibiotics for an infection or Ritalin to manage behaviour, and training is needed to know how and when to administer various drugs – and good quality training *is* a key to raising staff confidence. As many adults as possible need to be trained to be sure that someone is available at all times.

Other sensory supports

Once a child has moved beyond the foundation stage the curriculum begins to make increasing demands, especially on a child's ability to understand, read and write at an appropriate level. Where pupils are unable to meet these demands, the school needs to find other more creative ways of delivering the curriculum. The good news is that experience has taught us that additional sensory supports will help all the class, not just those pupils with learning difficulties.

Visual supports

Visual supports include objects, photographs, drawings, symbols, signing, text and moving images. Never underestimate the power of pictures or objects. Film is an important medium because it is so visual. Silent movies deliver just as powerful a message as films with sound – sometimes even more so.

Visual languages such as symbols and signing support the development of reading and writing, and aid communication.

Symbols

We are surrounded by symbols in everyday life, from road signs to the symbol above the fast food restaurant. The use of symbols to support language and literacy builds on this natural pictorial communication. For pupils who have difficulties with literacy, symbols act as a bridge to comprehension and expression; they help to sequence words and ideas and free intellectual development from the constraints of reading and writing. In text, pictographic cues help pupils begin the decoding and encoding process. Symbols differ from text in that each concept is represented by one image rather than a group of phonemes, for example:

There are many words that have more than one meaning. By using symbols the intended meaning can be represented accurately. For example:

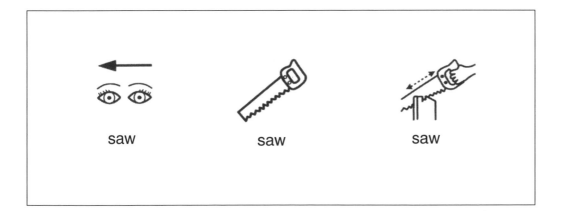

Symbols:

- are internationally recognised;
- overcome language barriers;
- are pictorial or abstract; and
- communicate ideas quickly and simply.

Symbolic development

Many symbols are iconic and easily recognisable, but others are abstract. Pupils need to learn the meaning of an abstract symbol in real contexts. For instance, the symbol for 'dog' is a picture of a dog. Most children have experienced dogs in many different situations, and their understanding of the concept of 'dog' enables them to understand the symbol. The symbol for 'over' is abstract, however, and the pupil will need to learn the meaning of this symbol in real situations. The symbol for 'over' might be introduced when the child is climbing over a bench or jumping over a puddle, so teaching the meaning of the symbol in a real-life context.

The understanding of symbols is hierarchical. Before their understanding can be assumed, children need to understand a symbol in more than one context. The progression for symbolic development is as follows:

- real objects
- representative objects
- photographs
- coloured pictures/drawings and line drawings
- standardised symbol systems
- written words.

Real objects

Real objects exist in three dimensions – they can be touched, held and turned. They have form, size and textures, and they can have taste and smell. When at early stages of development children need to have the symbol or sign introduced at the same time as they experience the object.

Objects are a powerful tool for supporting speech and text. Sensory boxes linked to texts bring words to life. Pupils who find reading challenging can access texts through a combination of audio tape, pictures and objects. In this way, pupils at the early stages of reading development are able to access age-appropriate texts alongside their peers.

Representative objects

Representative objects are the next level of symbolic development. These are usually miniature objects, like a small plastic animal or a toy vacuum cleaner. The pupil should understand that the miniature or toy object represents something real, for example, that a small plastic dog is a representation of a real dog.

Photographs

Photographs are usually the first two-dimensional representation presented to children. The change from 2D to 3D can pose for some children real perceptual difficulties, and at first photographs will need to be presented in conjunction with either the real object or a representative object.

Photographs should to be used with caution because they can be very confusing. Pupils with learning difficulties are often given photographic timetables in school. Problems arise when photographs in the timetable are of the focus pupil working in different classrooms, with one photograph looking very much like another. Where photographs contain too much visual information, pupils will not be able to differentiate what is important and what is not. If photographs are used they need to be of one object, or of one person on a plain background. Any more information will confuse pupils.

Box 4.1	**A sensory box for *Handa's Surprise* by Eileen Browne**

You will need:

- a copy of the text;
- one each of the different fruits mentioned in the story, preferably real;
- a length of patterned fabric;
- a straw basket;
- symbols for each fruit, the animals, and girl.

Children could be wrapped in the fabric and invited to hold the straw basket. As each of the fruits is mentioned; one is placed in the straw basket and the child is given the opportunity to hold, feel and smell each one. At the end of the story the basket can be passed around the class for all to look at and hold. If the fruits are real they can then be cut up and tasted by the whole class, made into a fruit salad or eaten as healthy snacks.

 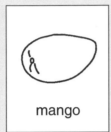 

tangerine   mango   banana

monkey   elephant

Handa's Surprise is published by Walker Books.

CASE STUDY	**Philip**

Philip has Autistic Spectrum Disorder. His visual timetable is made up of photographs, one of which is of the minibus that brings him to school. Every time Philip sees the photograph he says, 'baa'. No-one can understand why he says this, nor will he say 'bus' or 'home' when he sees the photo. After several weeks, a teaching assistant notices a speck in the corner of the photo. Under a magnifying glass the speck is found to be a sheep in the distance. She cuts around the minibus in the photo and mounts it on card. Philip now says 'bus' when shown the picture of the minibus.

Coloured pictures/drawings and line drawings

If pupils are to use symbols and signs successfully they need to understand that a drawing represents a real object or situation. The drawings need to be clear and simple, with little or no background detail. If a pupil has experienced either a real dog or a toy dog, they will know that a dog has four legs, two ears, two eyes and a tail. The drawing may show the dog sitting down or in profile, in which case the pupil has to take his or her knowledge of a dog and translate that knowledge into the two-dimensional image of the picture (as below). This picture shows only two obvious legs, and neither a tail nor any ears or eyes. For adults this is obviously a dog, but this will be much less clear to children with learning difficulties. Such a picture would need to be introduced alongside representative objects or photographs.

Standardised symbol systems

Standardised symbols are the first clear link with reading. Just as a word has to represent a whole genus, so does a symbol. For example, a pupil may have a pet German shepherd dog at home but a photograph can show an individual poodle; the symbol has to represent all dogs, from Great Danes to Jack Russells. Understanding this shift is an important developmental milestone.

There are a number of symbol systems that are used in schools. It does not matter which system is used, but it is important to decide on one and stick to it, to avoid confusion. Writing with Symbols 2000 software from Widgit has several symbol systems available that can be created easily just by typing in the words. To support communication the symbols can then be used in grids or to support text.

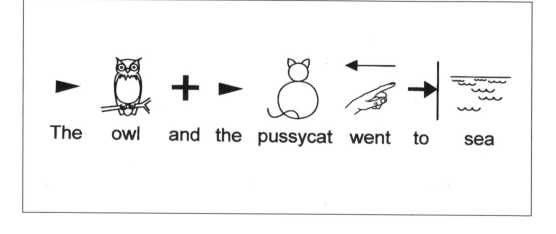

Written words

Understanding of the written word is the goal for all pupils. Symbols support reading development by giving visual cues above or below the words and help to develop left to right tracking. If symbols are colour coded they can be used to give pupils an understanding of sentence structure.

Here are some ideas on how to use symbols to support individuals and groups of pupils:

Visual timetables

Visual timetables are easy to make, and, to pupils with learning difficulties, give vital support and will in no way be detrimental to the rest of the class. Add symbols to the usual school timetable or mount onto a card and fix to a board with Velcro. This has the advantage of being easy to alter should any changes occur, such as rehearsals for the nativity play or a visiting music group.

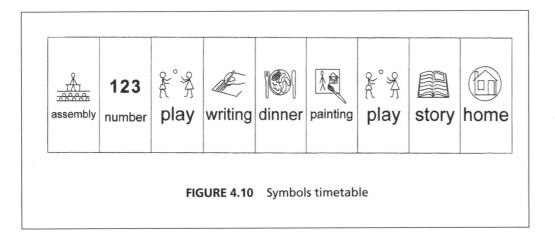

FIGURE 4.10   Symbols timetable

Communication boards

Communication boards are valuable tools in the classroom. They are very effective but unobtrusive. The boards are organised in a grid format containing the pupil's most commonly used symbols. These can be general symbols such as 'toilet', 'drink', 'hurt', 'yes' and 'no', as well as symbols for different subjects and/or photographs of key people. Bear in mind that it is important to teach new symbols *before* they are added to a communication board. If the board is kept on the desk, the pupil, teacher or teaching assistant can point to the relevant symbol or photograph to support communication.

Communication books

A cheap A5 peel-back photograph album is ideal for this purpose. The pages hold a selection of small symbol cards, and a strip of Velcro on the front cover holds the pupil's chosen symbol sequence.

   The book can also be used by the adults working with the pupil to support understanding, and to let the pupil know what is to happen next.

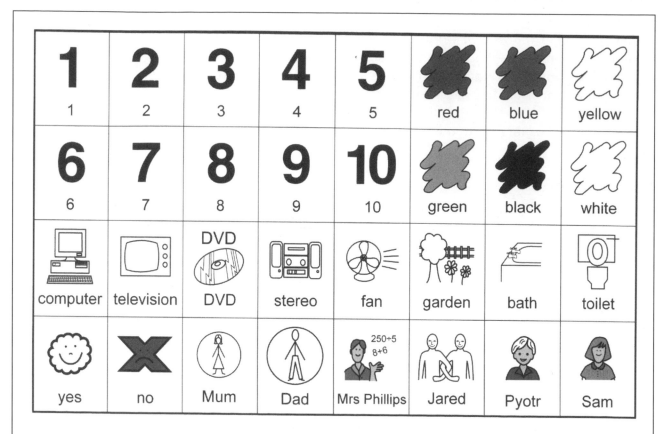

FIGURE 4.11   Communication board

PECS

The Picture Exchange Communication System (PECS) is a symbol system that is available commercially. It incorporates both a communication book and boards. Included is a basic range of symbols with additional symbols available for purchase. Information about PECS is available from Pyramid Educational Consultants Ltd on www.pecs.org.uk.

Access to information

As pupils move towards adolescence they need access to a wider range of important information. This information is usually text based: safety information, mobile telephone instructions, recipes for food technology, menus in restaurants, games instructions etc. This vital information is easily translated into symbols by using Writing with Symbols 2000 software. Some information may even save a life, such as the instructions on how to use a fire extinguisher. Symbol access to this information gives a measure of independence, develops self-advocacy, and enables children to begin to make their own life choices.

Memory mats

For pupils who need visual reminders for commonly-used information, memory mats are a valuable resource. A mat is made of a piece of A3 card with space for a book marked out in the centre. Around the edge of the mat are written the letters of the alphabet, days of the week, months of the year, and numbers and number words to ten – and any information that will support the pupil and aid

Safety information

Cross the road at the zebra crossing.

FIGURE 4.12 Symbol safety information

independent working. The mats will last for a long time if they are laminated but they can be amended regularly, perhaps to add new key words, if saved as a template on the computer.

1	2	3	4	5	6	7	8	9	10
one two three four five six seven eight nine ten		the		a		are		+ add - take away subtract	
		at		come		go		X times	
		get		Mum		Dad		= equals same as	

a b c d e f g h i j k l m n o p q r s t u v w x y z

FIGURE 4.13 An example of a memory mat

Signing

Just as symbols are all around us, so all of us to some extent use signs – but we call it gesture. We point, we touch and we wave our arms around. Many people find it impossible to communicate effectively without using their hands. Gesture is a means of adding nuance to speech, and it helps listeners to understand.

Less than 10 per cent of our understanding of language comes from the words we hear. The remainder of our understanding comes from the context, facial expression, body language, tone of voice and gesture. Children with learning difficulties often have difficulty both understanding *and* using the full range of communicative skills. They may be able to use facial expression, but might not understand the subtle, sophisticated changes between a smile and a sneer – a small facial movement that makes a huge difference to meaning.

Signing supports communication for pupils with learning difficulties by giving them a visual support for understanding speech, and by enabling them to make themselves better understood. Signing provides the means for them to let others know what they think about things at home and at school. Impaired communication excludes these children further from the social aspects of school life and extra-curricular activities.

Signing provides support to help pupils interact with each other in a relaxed way and to share experiences. Teaching all the school to sign one or two songs for the Christmas carol service will boost both the self-esteem of pupils with learning difficulties and the signing skills of the whole community. As part of the concert, teach the congregation the signs for the chorus of one of the carols – it's a moving sight to see a large number of people signing together.

There are several signing systems in use in the United Kingdom. The two systems most commonly used in mainstream schools are Signalong (www.signa-long.org.uk) and Makaton (www.makaton.org). Both are based on British Sign Language (BSL), and are sign-supporting systems that follow English word order. The primary purpose of these signing systems is to assist communication in cases of language difficulties associated with learning disabilities (Kennard 1997).

Parents are sometimes concerned that their child will stop trying to speak if they are taught to sign, but in fact the opposite is the case. Signing supports and also encourages children to speak, and signs are only ever used as an addition to speech. As with symbols, pupils gradually build up a vocabulary of signs, and start with commonly used words, such as mummy, good, hello, book. Again as with symbols, signs must be taught with real objects or in real situations if pupils are to attach the correct meaning to the sign.

If signing is to be effective and useful, other people in school need to be able to sign at the same level as the pupil with learning difficulties. This will involve training for parents, teachers, teaching assistants, and also other pupils. An ideal way to introduce signing is to teach the whole school community. Regular signing assemblies or lunchtime signing clubs are always popular.

Schools that have developed the use of signing find there are benefits for a large number of pupils: those with minor hearing loss caused by colds or glue ear, pupils with receptive language difficulties and pupils with attention disorders. A visual component added to speech will not impede more able pupils and will support many others. Signing has the extra benefit of slowing down speech; as only a very skilled signer can sign at the rate at which people usually talk. Signing also encourages adults to use more simplified and direct language.

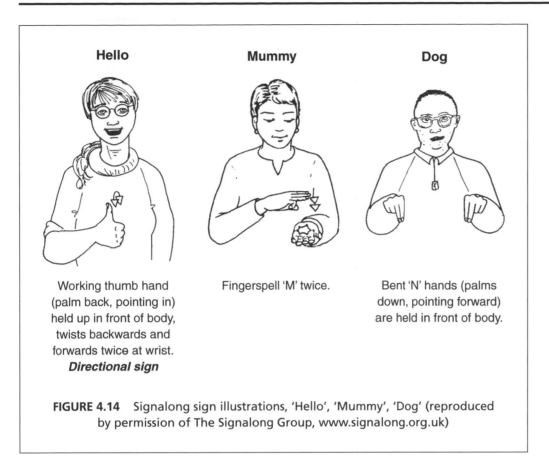

Hello

Working thumb hand (palm back, pointing in) held up in front of body, twists backwards and forwards twice at wrist.
Directional sign

Mummy

Fingerspell 'M' twice.

Dog

Bent 'N' hands (palms down, pointing forward) are held in front of body.

FIGURE 4.14   Signalong sign illustrations, 'Hello', 'Mummy', 'Dog' (reproduced by permission of The Signalong Group, www.signalong.org.uk)

Signing:

- supports receptive and expressive communication;
- is a valuable skill for all;
- slows down and simplifies speech;
- encourages independence and self-advocacy;
- enables communication between peers;
- increases participation in school life for pupils with learning difficulties.

Computers

Ten years ago the hope was that all children with communication or learning difficulties would have access to individual computers that would speak and write for them. Taking rather longer than was originally thought, the technology is now available to give appropriate technological support to facilitate pupils' communication and help them to access the curriculum.

Laptop computers

For pupils with learning difficulties, laptop computers loaded with a talking word processor or Clicker 5 increase independence. Adding other software will support learning across the curriculum and meet individual needs. Software such as concept mapping, maths and spelling programs also help pupils to develop basic skills. There are a number of low-cost computers available which are robust and ideal for use in the classroom. Pupils learn how to use the machines quickly, and then are better able to take a full part in lessons. Self-esteem is also improved, especially for older primary pupils. All information is easily transferred to printers or desktop computers, so creating a record of progress across the curriculum.

Be cautious when introducing computer-based learning to pupils with Autistic Spectrum Disorder (ASD). Pupils with ASD can be reluctant to stop working on the computer, or will refuse to work on the programs decided by the teacher. This may become a trigger for challenging behaviour. One way to avoid this situation is to give the pupil a visual schedule for the lesson, and to put the computer session at the end. The schedule shows the pupil what he/she is expected to do before using the computer. This system also has the added benefit of motivating a pupil to finish the other work first. A symbol showing what is to happen next, such as play, lunch or home time, will encourage the pupil to finish working at the computer without fuss.

CASE STUDY	Grace

Grace is in Year 4. She loves working on the computer and is constantly asking to use the desktop in the classroom. When she is allowed to use the computer she becomes very excited, and it is very difficult to persuade her to move to another activity. Grace's teacher devised a raffle ticket system to help Grace keep her enthusiasm for the computer within reasonable bounds. At the start of each day Grace was given four raffle tickets. Each ticket could be exchanged for ten minutes at the computer, a kitchen timer being used to let Grace know when her time was up.

On the first day, Grace used all her tickets within the first lesson and cried for the rest of the day when she was not allowed another go on the computer. On the second day, she used up the tickets in the morning, but accepted that she could not use the computer in the afternoon. Within a week Grace had learned to space out her requests over a day, and no longer made a fuss when it was time to stop. Her teacher introduced a computer symbol into her daily schedule and she no longer needs the raffle tickets.

Switches

Switches are used with computers to replace a keyboard keystroke or mouse click. Switches can be used at a basic level to develop a pupil's understanding of cause and effect by changing images on a screen through pressing the switch. Using scanning, switches give pupils access to a wide range of software. Scanning is a switch technique in which a program highlights available choices one at a time. By activating a switch the pupil makes a choice when the item they wish to choose is highlighted. The choices available may be just two items, or may be more complex choices that allow pupils to control all the functions of the computer. Switches enable pupils for their own use to operate electrical equipment, such as a fan or a CD player.

Some switches can be used as communication devices. 'Big Mack' switches record a message that can be replayed as many times as the pupil presses the switch.

FIGURE 4.15 Big Mack switch

Resources

Under Part 4 of the Disability Discrimination Act 1995, schools are not required to make physical alterations to buildings and the physical environment. These requirements are covered by the longer-term planning duties for LEAs and schools. Nor are schools required to provide auxiliary educational aids and services, or specialist equipment that is necessary to meet a child's identified needs. For example, this would include a radio microphone for a pupil with a severe hearing impairment. Outside these exemptions, however, there is a range of equipment that all primary schools are reasonably expected to have available to support learning. Much of this equipment is comparatively low cost, and usefully supports many pupils with both temporary and permanent difficulties:

- sloping writing surfaces;
- non-slip mats;
- adjustable height chairs;
- triangular pen and pencil grips;
- easy-grip scissors;
- stress balls.

Software:
- Writing With Symbols 2000 (Widgit Software), www.widget.co.uk
- Inclusive Writer (Inclusive Technology), www.inclusive .co.uk
- Clicker 5 (Crick Computing), www.cricksoft.com
- Kidspiration (Inclusive Technology)
- Life Skills (Inclusive Technology)
- WordShark (Inclusive Technology)
- NumberShark (Inclusive Technology)
- IEP Manager (SEMERC), www.semerc.com

Access devices:
- Trackerball
- Joystick
- Switches
- Big Mack communication device

Information and support on the above hardware and software is available from companies such as Inclusive Technology and SEMERC, who have consultants who are also qualified and experienced teachers. The consultants will visit schools to offer expert advice and training to staff.

Support toolboxes

Some schools provide their teaching assistants with support toolboxes. These small toolboxes might contain a variety of equipment to support pupils in lessons. Much of the equipment in the toolbox is easily available in school, but it is more time-efficient to have it all together and to hand.
The toolbox could contain:

camera	audio tape	stress ball	stamps
bulldog clip	paper fasteners	Blu-tack	rubber bands
stapler	colouring pad	skipping rope	dominoes
sticky tape	treasury tags	Velcro™	Dictaphone
pens and pencils	plastic wallets	sticky labels	pencil sharpener
small ruler	coloured pens	floppy disks	glue
paper clips	triangular grips	highlighter pens	counters
scissors	rubbers	calculator	dice or spinners
tissues	sand timer	self-adhesive notes	playing cards

FIGURE 4.16 Suggested contents of Support Toolbox

Outside agencies

Professionals from other agencies are a fantastic source of information and ideas for support for pupils with learning difficulties. Some professionals, such as occupational therapists, may work directly with parents. Parents will usually pass on booklets and/or therapy programmes that can be incorporated into staff training or the school timetable. Always try to obtain a copy of a pupil's therapy targets, even if the therapy takes place in clinic or at home.

When planning annual review meetings, invite all the professionals who work with the pupil. The primary purpose of the meeting is to review the pupil's Statement of Special Educational Needs, but the meeting is an ideal forum to share information and advice, and will help professionals from outside education gain an understanding of how the pupil is being included in the school. The nature and level of support can be discussed and amended to give the child more help, to develop peer support, or to plan for increased independence.

Summary

When planning support for inclusion, see if you can find additional, more creative ways of supporting pupils who have learning difficulties. Utilising other adults and peer support, as well as teaching assistants and teachers, is not only more effective in practice, it's more cost effective too. The pupil who has learning difficulties benefits from being part of a wider social circle that demands and develops different social skills. Let's consign the practice of teaching assistants sitting next to pupils in all lessons – the 'Velcro' teaching assistant – to history!

Chapter 5 looks at how assessment can be used to support inclusion.

5

Assessment to support inclusion: including the P scales

Government initiatives drop through school post boxes with alarming regularity. Sometimes these initiatives merely add to the bureaucratic burden; sometimes a real gem slips through almost unnoticed. The P scales are just such a gem. Designed originally to facilitate whole-school target-setting for special schools, the P scales are a perfect assessment tool for tracking the attainment of individuals and of groups of pupils. They provide a common vocabulary for assessing pupils in all settings, but many mainstream schools still do not realise what a valuable aid P scales can be.

The P scales are important and powerful. Important because they are the first attempt to link the attainments of pupils with more significant learning difficulties directly to the National Curriculum; powerful because they support mainstream schools in meeting and assessing the needs of pupils with learning difficulties. Together with the Guidelines for Planning, Teaching and Assessing the Curriculum for Pupils with Learning Difficulties (QCA 2001), the P scales give schools excellent advice and support on including pupils working below level one of the National Curriculum.

What does the P stand for?

The P scales are designed to measure the attainment of pupils working below Level 1 of the National Curriculum. The original P (performance criteria) scales document was published by the Qualifications and Curriculum Authority (QCA) in 1998 (revised in 2001), and was designed to support the target-setting process for individuals and schools in English, mathematics and science. The Guidelines for Planning, Teaching and Assessing the Curriculum for Pupils with Learning Difficulties (QCA 2001), were published three years later and include P scales from P1 to P8 in all National Curriculum subjects, PSHE (Personal, Social and Health Education), Citizenship and Religious Education. They are a valuable resource for all schools and particularly useful where schools need to demonstrate value-added attainment for pupils with learning difficulties. Knowledge and understanding of the P scales could be a part of schools' anticipatory response to Part 4 of the Disability Discrimination Act (1995) as set out in the Disability Rights Commission Code of Practice for Schools (Disability Rights Commission 2002).

The P scales provide eight descriptions that lead up to Level 1 of the National Curriculum, termed P1 to P8. The performance descriptions for P1 to P3 are common across all subjects, and are designed for pupils with profound and multiple learning difficulties who need to access the curriculum through sensory activities and experiences. There are two differentiated descriptions within each of levels P1 to P3, termed (i) and (ii) within each level.

For example, in science:

P2 (i) Pupils begin to respond consistently to familiar people, events and objects. They react to new activities and experiences, *for example, discarding objects with unfamiliar textures.* They begin to show interest in people, events and objects, *for example, leaning forward to follow the scent of a crushed herb.* They accept and engage in co-operative exploration with the help of another, *for example, feeling materials in hand-over-hand partnerships with a member of staff.*

P2 (ii) Pupils begin to be proactive in their interactions. They communicate consistent preferences and affective responses, *for example, showing a consistent dislike for certain flavours or textures.* They recognise familiar people, events and objects, *for example, moving towards particular features of familiar environments.* They perform actions, often by trial and error, and they remember learned responses over short periods of time, *for example, rejecting food items after recent experience of bitter flavours.* They co-operate with shared exploration and supported participation, *for example, examining materials handed to them.* (QCA/DfES 2001)

The text in italics shows subject specific examples.

The P scales in English and mathematics each have three differentiated descriptions leading to Level 1 of the National Curriculum. The elements in English are:

- speaking (expressive communication) and listening (receptive communication);
- reading; and
- writing.

In maths the elements are:

- using and applying mathematics;
- numbers; and
- space, shape and measures.

The English and maths criteria are consistent with the Primary National Strategy, and enable teachers to track back from the frameworks into the P scales. It is then possible to identify objectives appropriate to a pupil's current level of ability which can be addressed in age-appropriate contexts (see Chapter 3). P8 reflects the performance described in the Early Learning Goals and Reception objectives in the Early Years Framework for Teaching.

How can the P scales be used in mainstream primary schools?

The P scales give mainstream schools the tools needed to set appropriate and achievable targets for pupils with learning difficulties, and to record small steps of progress. They provide a framework of common performance measures for benchmark information, and for the calculation of value-added improvement for pupils working at these levels (QCA/DfES 2001). They support the detailed assessment of pupil attainment for reports and annual reviews, and offer ready-made objectives for individual education plans.

When used alongside the frameworks for literacy and numeracy, P scales give teachers a means of differentiating work for classes that include children with a wide range of ability. They provide objectives appropriate to the abilities of a pupil with learning difficulties which may then be taught in age-related contexts with age-appropriate resources.

Where schools have a cohort of pupils working below or within Level 1 of the National Curriculum, the P scales can be used as part of the whole-school target-setting process. Where schools do not have sufficient numbers of pupils working below Level 1, they may create a cohort of pupils with learning difficulties by working with other local schools. This has an added bonus of allowing staff to compare pupils' progress, and to share ideas and resources.

The P scales across the curriculum

The curriculum guidance documents – Planning, Teaching and Assessing the Curriculum for Pupils with Learning Difficulties (QCA 2001) – include P scales P1 to P8 for all National Curriculum subjects, PSHE, Citizenship and Religious Education.

These documents are meant as guidance only, but provide a sound foundation for planning, target-setting and assessment. They give ideas for ensuring progression and age-appropriate experiences. In addition they give advice and offer strategies for teaching pupils with a diverse range of needs.

Assessment

The P scales are an ideal assessment tool to use with pupils who have learning difficulties. They provide small steps towards and within Level 1 of the National Curriculum, and can be used as either subject or IEP targets. Several publications are available that break down the P scales into smaller steps suitable for pupils with more significant learning difficulties. Some of these commercial publications include grids for recording attainment and progression over time. The grids are useful as evidence of attainment and progression, but remember that the P scales do not in themselves constitute a curriculum. It is not enough for pupils simply to work through the P scale objectives, either on their own or in a small group.

P scale objectives need to be taught in the context of the child's year group class, with age-appropriate experiences and resources.

The P scales and English

The P scales for English are divided into three components:

- speaking and listening;
- reading;
- writing.

These components tally with the literacy strands in the National Primary Strategy. The National Literacy Strategy has produced a Strand Tracker document for non-fiction objectives (NLS 2002) (available online at www.standards.dfes.gov.uk/literacy/publications) that shows individual strands of the literacy framework from Year 6 to reception. Strand trackers are particularly useful when tracking back for objectives to link with later years of the framework. This enables teachers in primary schools to track back through the literacy framework and into the appropriate P scale matching the pupil's level of attainment. In Key Stage 2, when teaching English to pupils with learning difficulties, it is necessary to ensure progression in terms of context and materials, as well as skills. Pupils can access some elements of most texts, or related or adapted texts could be used. Several publications now offer adapted texts based on Key Stage 2 books. These publications include passages of simplified and symbol supported text. They also include lists of sensory resources that can be used to support access to the texts for pupils with profound and multiple learning difficulties.

Ntikuma went home

with the drum

and no beans for mum.

FIGURE 5.1   Example of symbol supported text from *Tumpa Tumpa* (Walker *et al.* 2002)

The P scales and maths

The P scales for mathematics also are divided into three components:

- using and applying mathematics;
- numbers; and
- shape, space and measures.

Excellent materials have been produced by the Primary Strategy based on the maths framework and the P scales. Especially useful is the document Towards the National Curriculum for Mathematics in Key Stages 1 and 2 (DfES 2002) which gives examples of what pupils with SEN should be able to do at each P level. This document is designed to be used alongside the primary framework. The materials make tracking back relatively quick and simple and can be obtained from primary maths consultants or on the DfES website at www.standards. dfes.gov.uk/numeracy/communities/inclusion. Offering pupils a wide range of active and relevant maths experiences is important for maintaining motivation and attention. Applying mathematical concepts in real-life contexts helps pupils to generalise skills and consolidates their understanding.

The power of positive target-setting

Setting targets is the only way to be sure of meeting the particular learning needs of children with learning difficulties. Positive targets that are achievable within a realistic timescale drive forward both progress and attainment. The pupil knows what he/she is expected to learn, and by when. The teacher and teaching assistant can measure progress easily, and adjust targets, teaching methods and support to match the pupil's changing learning needs. If merely *present* in lessons that are not differentiated, and for which the child has no individual objectives, he/she will learn very little. With positive targets that are addressed in the lessons through differentiated activities and resources, and based on the key concepts method or curriculum overlapping (see Chapter 3), the teacher can be confident that the needs of the pupil with learning difficulties are addressed.

The power of positive target-setting lies in a child's sense of achievement and success. For a pupil who may rarely experience the feeling of pride in their work, realistic targets will guarantee success. Celebrating that success each time the pupil achieves their target will build motivation to try harder the next time. Targets may not be the same as those for everyone else, but they are no less important or effective for that. Socially and educationally, the 'cycle of success' can transform a pupil.

Small steps to success

Attainments made by children with learning difficulties are no less valid than those of other pupils. The progress made may be in small steps, but that progress is gained through enormous effort and determination.

What is meant here by success?

For pupils with learning difficulties, success can mean making progress against realistic IEP and subject targets. It may mean being independent in class. It might mean making friends and maintaining relationships. The P scales support this success when used as a scaffold to help both the school and the pupil move forward. With the P scales, teachers are able to identify the next small step, and at the end of a school year they can look back and see just how far the pupil has travelled. Delight when a child achieves P8 and moves into Level 1 of the National Curriculum is no less real for a pupil in Year 6 than for a child in the foundation stage.

More than 'working towards'

Until the advent of the P scales, pupils with learning difficulties were often assessed at 'W' – working towards Level 1 – for their entire school careers. No matter how much real progress pupils made, that progress could not be reflected in terms of National Curriculum attainment. Parents would become demoralised to see 'W' on annual reports year after year, causing them sometimes to question whether their child had made any worthwhile progress at all.

When in 1998 the first P scales document was published this was all changed. At last teachers could show progression leading into the National Curriculum, and parents could see their children on the same track as others. The P scales gave a common framework and language for assessment for all pupils. At last special schools could measure what they valued, and celebrate just how much progress was being made by their pupils.

IEP targets

The P scales for English and mathematics may be used very effectively as the basis of targets for individual education plans. Each of the level descriptions contains a number of sentences that can either be used individually or joined together to create an IEP target. For example:

> Georgina in Year 6 is working at P7 in English and maths. Georgina has a speech and language disorder, and a general developmental delay.

English: Writing:

> P7: Pupils group letters and leave spaces between them as though they are writing separate words. Some letters are correctly formed. They are aware of the sequence of letters, symbols and words. (QCA/DfES 2001:25)

An IEP target based on this P scale for Georgina in Year 6 could be:

> Georgina will spell her first and last names correctly.

Maths: Numbers:

> P7: Pupils join in rote counting to ten. They count at least five objects reliably. They begin to recognise numerals from 1 to 5 and to understand that each represents a constant number or amount. They respond appropriately to key vocabulary and questions. Pupils begin to recognise differences in quantity. In practical situations they respond to 'add one' and 'take one'. (QCA 2001)

An IEP target based on this P scale for Georgina in Year 6 could be:

> Georgina will recognise numerals 1 to 5 and link numerals to sets of objects.

The P scales for Personal, Social and Health Education and Citizenship can be used to inform IEP targets for PSHE. This linkage will give teachers an understanding of the comparative level of a pupil's social functioning.

Georgina has particular difficulties in the area of PSHE, and her IEP target is based on P6:

> Pupils respond to others in group situations, playing or working in a small group co-operatively, for example, taking turns appropriately.

Georgina's IEP target in this area is:

> Georgina will wait for her turn in circle time activities.

Using the P scales to plan for progression

Progress is not always linear – onwards, upwards, better! For pupils with learning difficulties we may have to re-examine just what we mean by progress. Progress can mean learning new skills, but it could also mean practising, maintaining and extending existing skills. Pupils with learning difficulties continue to learn and make progress throughout their lives. The myth that pupils with learning difficulties reach a 'plateau' in their learning, and subsequently learn nothing more is just that – a myth. As with all children, pupils facing additional challenges such as family breakdown or illness will have a slower rate of progress. When pupils are making significant progress in one area, sometimes the rate of development of other skills may slow down.

No matter how wonderful our teaching may be, or how many targets we set, there will be a progressively widening gap between the attainment of children with significant learning difficulties and other pupils. The answer to this is not to propose that the pupil should go somewhere else because they cannot cope with a mainstream curriculum. There should not be an assumption that pupils will all progress at the same rate. The answer is to accept the widening gap – often easier for teachers than for parents – and then to discount it. It is unnecessary and unfair continually to compare pupils' levels of ability. What matters is that pupils make adequate progress against the targets set for them as individuals in IEPs and in the curriculum subjects.

The general guidelines (QCA 2001) recommend that planning for progression for individuals or groups might focus on:

Developing skills

As well as learning new skills, pupils with learning difficulties need more opportunities:

- to revisit skills learned previously;
- to generalise learned skills into different contexts; and
- to practise and maintain skills.

For example, pupils will learn to count to ten in maths, and this skill can be practised in music, PE, design and technology, and art.

Curricular content

As pupils move through the primary phase, it is necessary to ensure they have access to new knowledge and experiences. The breadth of the learning experiences should not be limited because of their learning difficulties. A broadening curriculum throughout Key Stage 2 will extend pupils' knowledge and understanding. A developing awareness of personal, health, ethical and environmental issues will help pupils begin to make informed decisions about their own lives. For instance, an understanding of healthy eating may help a pupil make changes in his/her eating patterns, and so avoid potential health problems in later life.

Contexts for learning

Teachers can support progression by planning opportunities for pupils to apply skills, knowledge and understanding in new contexts. Giving pupils access to a variety of experiences, activities and environments appropriate to their chronological ages, interests and prior achievement helps them to generalise skills and understanding. Tracking back to find appropriate objectives from earlier Key Stages should then be linked to age-appropriate contexts. For example, a pupil in Year 5 working on objectives from Year R of the Numeracy Strategy in maths would not learn how to use a calculator *unless* the Year R objectives were taught in the context of the Year 5 lesson. This is because the use of calculators is not included in the framework for Year R.

Resources

Access to a differing range of resources over time in a school is an important part of progression. Pupils with learning difficulties will become bored if they are expected always to work with infant books and equipment. At the start of Year 3 teachers can work together to identify a progression of resources in each subject. For example, 'Compare Bears' may be appropriate for counting and sorting in the infants, but in the juniors children need to use a range of other, more age-appropriate tools for these tasks, such as:

Year 3: Stickle bricks, shells
Year 4: Unifix cubes, Lego bricks
Year 5: counters, buttons, washers
Year 6: coins, dominoes, playing cards

Teaching methods and support

As the pupil with learning difficulties moves through the school, progression may be shown in the form of differing methods of teaching and support. These differences will be determined by pupils' individual strengths and learning styles. Pupils need to begin to learn how to monitor and improve their own learning. Gradually they may take shared responsibility for setting their learning goals, and for deciding what to keep in their Experience Folders. This progression towards greater independence is particularly important towards the end of Key Stage 2 as part of the preparation for transfer to secondary school.

To show progression, the style and level of support received by a pupil could be changed. A very 'hands-on' model of support may be appropriate in Key Stage 1, but in Key Stage 2 increasingly pupils should be expected to work independently. A gradual reduction in the level of adult support, and a greater expectation of co-operative work with other pupils, will support progression towards independence.

Problem solving

Everyone needs to develop problem solving skills, but pupils with learning difficulties have very few opportunities to solve problems either individually or in groups. Pupils can be dependent on adult support and so reluctant to try new things, or sometimes it is considered that they are not able to contribute to group activities involving problem solving. Children with learning difficulties must be encouraged to take risks and try new things. Sometimes they will make mistakes, but making mistakes and learning from them is a vital part of learning. To develop the skills of problem solving, start with individual or paired tasks based on real everyday activities. A visual or object framework in which to operate will give the pupil the support they need.

CASE STUDY — **Darren**

Darren is in Year 4 at his village primary school. The school is having a Halloween party and Darren's class has been given the task of devising party games. Darren and his friend Kieran are asked to organise the 'Bobbing for Apples' game with support from Mrs Jones, Darren's TA. The boys watch a video of children playing the game and Mrs Jones has made a symbols list showing them what they need to collect. With help from Mrs Jones, the boys devised an action plan:

1. Find a bowl – put it on Kieran's head to see if it is big enough.
2. Count how many tennis balls fit into the bowl, so Mrs Jones knows how many apples to buy.
3. Fill the bowl with water. Should they take the bowl to the sink and carry it back to the table, or should they use a jug to fill it?

The combination of visual support and help from Mrs Jones meant that Darren and Kieran were able successfully to do their bit for the party. This kind of activity has a huge impact on the self-esteem of children with learning difficulties, and enhances their role as part of the school community.

Setting small problems within other activities, where the pupil has to work something out to be able to continue, will help to begin the problem solving process. For example, in a science lesson on electricity the resources box contains everything the pupil needs to make a circuit, except a battery. The pupil has a diagram that shows the battery. She looks in the neighbouring box and checks the contents. Realising what is missing, she asks the teacher for a battery.

This small problem gave the pupil reasons to think, check, investigate, interact and communicate. Involving pupils who have learning difficulties in group problem solving activities will further develop these skills. In group activities, such as treasure hunts around the school using picture and written clues, other pupils will model thinking and problem-solving skills. Seeing and hearing how other people work things out is also an important part of the learning process.

Progression for pupils with profound and multiple learning difficulties

Pupils with profound and multiple learning difficulties (PMLD) may need to work at the same level of the P scales for several years. Their progression needs to be planned in terms of experiences, resources and contexts. Many pupils with PMLD access the curriculum through all their senses, and need activities that involve active exploration:

- feeling different textures;
- experiencing different kinds of movement;
- tasting a range of foods;
- smelling perfumes, herbs and flowers;
- listening to music and environmental sounds;
- looking at, and through, colours and visual effects.

Linking these sensory activities to age-appropriate subject contexts will ensure progression. Trying to give these experiences in isolation creates a stagnant situation that is not stimulating, either for the child or for those adults working with the pupil.

CASE STUDY | **Charity**

Charity is in Year 1 and has profound and multiple learning difficulties. She communicates using eye-gaze and facial expression. One of her IEP targets is to maintain her head in an upright position. For most of each day Charity works with her TA in a large cupboard that has been turned into a small sensory room where she works on her IEP targets. However, one afternoon her teaching assistant was called away urgently and no-one was available to cover for her, so Charity had to join in the art lesson with her class. Several children asked to work with Charity and she smiled throughout the lesson as she made hand prints on paper. Her teacher noticed that she had held her head up throughout the lesson and she was much more alert than in the one-to-one situation in the sensory room.

P1 to P3

The earliest levels of the P scales, particularly P1 to P3, support schools in developing the curriculum to meet the needs of pupils with profound and multiple learning difficulties. The curriculum needs to give these pupils opportunities to develop their skills in:

- communication;
- interaction;
- understanding cause and effect;
- sensory awareness and perception;
- linking of objects, events and experiences;
- predicting and anticipating.

With a little thought and creativity, these activities can be built into lessons in mainstream primary schools. Below is an example of a pupil with profound and multiple learning difficulties included in a Year 3 music lesson.

CASE STUDY | **Saeed Year 3 Music**

QCA Scheme of work for music. Unit 9: Animal Magic: exploring descriptive sounds (QCA 2000)

Section 1: How can music describe different animals?

Saeed uses a wheelchair for all his time in school. He has always attended mainstream schools and loves the company of the boys in his class. Saeed communicates by eye pointing and smiling. He is working at level P2(ii) of the P scales in music.

P2(ii): Pupils begin to be proactive in their interactions. They communicate consistent preferences and affective responses. They recognise familiar people, events and objects. They perform actions, often by trial and improvement, and they remember learned responses over short periods of time. They co-operate with shared exploration and supported participation.

Saeed's objectives for the unit at P2(ii):

- to communicate consistent preferences by eye pointing (curriculum overlap);
- to link music/sounds with toy animals.

Background

Saeed accesses the curriculum through all his senses. While listening is the primary sense used here, the teacher and teaching assistant have collected toy animals that Saeed looks at and holds, to link to the short extracts of music which he hears. The other children in the class are involved in the same activity but they are using words and pictures of the animals.

The extracts of music are taken from the *Carnival of the Animals* by Saint-Saëns. The class work on this unit is planned to take half a term.

Sessions 1 and 2

As each extract of music is played, the appropriate soft toy is given to Saeed. The toys have been chosen because of their differing shapes and textures: fur, fabric, satin, feathers, snakeskin, etc.

Sessions 3 and 4

Saeed is seated in front of the six soft toys and as he reaches out for one the associated track on the CD is played. The other children in the class choose from pictures of the animals.

Session 5

Two toy animals are placed in front of Saeed. The toy he looks at, or reaches out for, is given to him and the CD track played. This process is then repeated with the other toy animals. Saeed's classmates listen to the music and match a picture of an animal to the extract.

Session 6

Saeed joins the rest of the class in a music and movement session to build on the listening skills they have developed over the unit. The children suggest and try out movements to match both the extracts and the animals – high, small, fast movements for 'The Aviary', and slow, low movements for 'The Tortoise'. Saeed's TA moves his wheelchair in time to the music or moves the toy animals in front of him.

Saeed's responses throughout the unit of work are recorded on digital camera and video. This evidence of his experiences is stored in his Experience Folder.

Physical, orientation and mobility skills

Pupils with profound and multiple learning difficulties will have additional priorities that have to be addressed in school, of physical, orientation and mobility skills. These skills include:

- fine motor skills, such as grasping, holding and manipulating;
- whole body skills, such as the co-ordination of movement, rolling and walking;
- positioning skills, such as head control;
- tolerating and/or managing mobility aids, such as a wheelchair, walking frame or splints.

These priorities can usually be addressed in mainstream classes without recourse to specialist equipment.

Fine motor skills can be developed in:

- art and design – working with a range of media and textures
- design and technology – joining components
- music – exploring and playing percussion instruments
- maths – creating different sizes of sets of objects.

Whole body skills can be developed in:

- drama – exploring different kinds of movement
- physical education – lying and sitting on the trampoline, gymnastics
- dance – exploring body shapes, moving in time to music.

Positioning skills, and tolerating and managing mobility aids, will be developed in all lessons and other school situations. Practising these priorities in the supported setting of a school will prepare children for the move to secondary school, and for living in their local community.

Pupils with additional medical priorities

The concept of progress may be more difficult to define for those pupils who have significant medical needs in addition to profound and multiple learning difficulties. For pupils with degenerative diseases, progress may need to be defined in terms of maintaining, rather than extending, skills and understanding. Progress and progression can be defined in terms of the breadth of the experiences in which the pupil is involved. In this situation the P scales offer an objective benchmark for assessment, and strategies for developing appropriate provision, such as the use of communication aids or ICT support for an individual pupil.

Individual Education Plans

What should an IEP look like?

No one has yet has produced an Individual Education Plan (IEP) format which is perfect for all situations. IEPs can be A5, A4, A3 or foolscap size. They can be landscape or portrait. They can be handwritten, typed, or word processed. What matters is that the format works in your school for your pupils and you use it consistently. When your school has agreed a format, it is then vital that all members of staff use it. The importance of this consistency should be made very clear to new members of staff who may bring with them a format used in their previous school. Inspectors and parents alike need to see IEPs that use a common format, that are clear, and that have direct relevance to the pupil's school experiences. It is a waste of time and effort to have IEPs sitting in a folder until they are brought out for review at the end of the term.

Individual Education Plans are working documents that need constantly to be at hand. Copies of IEPs should be distributed to each and every member of staff working with the student. Teachers and teaching assistants should be expected to scribble notes on them, to add post-its, and even cut and paste some sections; these additions make for dynamic documents that match a child's learning needs. If the IEP looks pristine when the time comes for review, then it has been a waste of time. All copies of the IEP should be collected in before the review, and the notes and jottings collated to give a more rounded assessment than could be gained from a single perspective.

Some large primary schools have a significant number of pupils at School Action and School Action Plus of the Code of Practice or who have statements. Generating effective IEPs for a large number of pupils is itself a barrier to effective provision for pupils with special educational needs. The burden of work is often unmanageable for a SENCO who is expected to write, monitor, and review IEP targets at least once a term, in addition to other teaching and pastoral duties. The advent of computer software, such as IEP Manager (SEMERC), has undoubtedly helped to speed up the process, but the statements in these programs often are insufficiently precise for pupils with more complex learning difficulties. Limit the number of targets to just three or four, as recommended by the SEN Code of Practice (DfES 2001), to keep the process manageable. Involve class teachers, teaching assistants and parents in the monitoring and review of the IEPs. This will share the work, and supports the professional development of colleagues.

The Special Educational Needs Code of Practice (DfES 2001) gives clear guidance on the precise information an IEP should include:

- short-term targets set by or for the pupil
- teaching strategies to be used
- the provision to be put into place
- when the plan is to be reviewed
- success and/or exit criteria
- outcomes (to be recorded when the IEP is reviewed). (DfES 2001:59)

'Additional to and different from'

The Code of Practice is very clear that an IEP should contain only targets that are additional to, or different from, the usual differentiated curriculum provision. Even where pupils are grouped in sets for literacy and numeracy, all teachers are expected to plan differentiated work and activities to match the varied learning needs of the class. The IEP should identify the different or additional provision, over and above the differentiated curriculum, which is to be offered to the child.

A good IEP will focus on three or four targets, and relate to key areas from communication, literacy, mathematics, physical skills, or aspects of behaviour and social skills.

Additional priorities

An IEP needs to address additional priorities for some pupils at certain times. These priorities may include organisation and study skills, such as:

- attending and directing attention;
- sustaining interest and motivation;
- selecting and organising their own environment;
- managing their own time;
- completing a task;
- taking responsibility for tasks.

For certain pupils personal and social skills may be an important prerequisite for learning. Areas such as personal care skills, managing their own behaviour and managing their own emotions, will be priorities for some pupils at different times (QCA 2001).

ICT skills, working with others and independence skills may be equally important for some children in inclusive settings (Tod 1999). These cross-curricular and cross-*situational* targets will have relevance across the curriculum, making it much more simple and effective both to address the targets and monitor progress. There is no requirement to set IEP targets in all areas of the curriculum. The targets must be directed at the skills or knowledge that the pupil needs most at any particular time.

Effective targets are those which are realistic and understood by the pupil, the pupil's parents, the class teacher and teaching assistants. It is advisable to keep targets simple, clear and free of any jargon. Many parents are reluctant to admit that they do not understand terminology used in IEPs. If they do not understand the IEP they will not be able to support their child. It is useful to write the IEP to the level of the understanding of the pupil. Ultimately it is the pupil who will achieve the targets, and really it is the pupil who needs to understand them. For some pupils this may mean using symbols to support the text, or having the targets spoken on audio tape, or signed and spoken on video.

Make sure that IEP targets are based upon what a pupil is expected to learn. It is surprising how many IEP targets are based on what teachers and teaching assistants will do, and so bypass the pupil altogether. A target such as '*Megan will have a one-to-one session for literacy every day*' does not require Megan to do or learn anything. Megan may well benefit from the daily session but this is really a target for her teacher. '*Megan will match the sounds to letters in her name*' is a target that Megan can work on over a limited period of time. She can work on this target in lots of lessons, and she can practice it with her parents for homework.

Annual review meetings

A pupil's Statement of Special Educational Needs is reviewed at the annual review meeting. This meeting is part of the statutory annual review process and involves parents, the class teacher, the SENCO, teaching assistants and, where feasible, the pupil. Even if the child stays for just a few minutes, it is always valuable to involve him/her in the meeting so as to be able to tell everyone about friends or favourite activities.

Invitations are sent out to therapists working with the pupil, to educational psychologists, LEA officers, and sometimes the child's paediatrician. Even when these professionals are not able to attend the meeting often they send written reports giving a basis for future targets. Copies of the child's current statement should be available for everyone who attends the meeting.

In addition to reviewing the statement, the annual review meeting will discuss the child's current IEP, and new or amended targets can be considered by those present. The people at the meeting should come together as a team to identify the areas of greatest need for the pupil over the following twelve months. The IEP targets can then be based on these overarching, long-term targets. In this way the overall shape of the individual education planning for the following year can be agreed and understood by all the key players. While the annual review meeting is separate from an IEP review, the opportunity of having pupil, parents, teachers, teaching assistants and professionals together is too good to miss. Linking long-term targets from the annual review to the short-term targets in the individual education plan will ensure continuity, and limit the number of extra targets on which a pupil is working.

Once the long-term targets are agreed at the annual review, the SENCO or class teacher can then:

- set short-term targets;
- identify how the targets are to be addressed (resources etc.);
- identify the school contexts in which the targets will be addressed (in-class, small group, one-to-one etc.);
- identify the people who will support the pupil in achieving the targets (peer support, teaching assistants, learning support service teachers etc.);
- identify how parents can support the pupil to achieve the targets;
- arrange monitoring procedures.

Ensure targets are sufficiently sharp, clear and unambiguous. The pupil should be able to go home and say,

'Guess what, Mum. Today I learned how to . . .',

or

'Today I learned that . . .'

Pupils and their parents are involved in the process if targets are written in this way, and they will be able to work together toward achieving the targets because they are shared and understood.

Individual behaviour plans

Where pupils have behaviour problems in addition to learning difficulties, there is a danger that either the behaviour targets on the IEP will force out curricular targets, or that the pupil is given both an individual behaviour plan *and* an IEP. The pupil then ends up with more targets than he/she can manage, and little will be achieved. Keeping a balance of curricular and behaviour targets within the IEP increases the likelihood that the targets will be achieved. Behaviour difficulties often improve dramatically when IEP targets are realistic and understood by, and shared with, the pupil and parents.

Beware of having targets on individual behaviour plans that are linked to a pupil's particular area of difficulty. For example, pupils with Attention Deficit Hyperactivity Disorder (ADHD) are often given targets related to reducing their impulsivity or sitting still in class. For many pupils with ADHD such targets are not achievable and so have failure in-built.

Pupil involvement

When pupils are involved in setting their own targets and monitoring their own progress, teachers and parents find that the pupil tries harder and is more motivated to succeed. Put pupils at the heart of the target-setting process and they are given a stake in their own learning. Children with learning difficulties can usually identify what they find hard in school, and where they would like to improve. Spend time with the pupil before the annual review meeting in order to talk about their successes and concerns. This helps to clarify the areas for development, and helps to prepare the pupil if he/she is to speak in the meeting. Chapter 8 goes into more detail about pupil participation.

IEP targets from other professionals

Pupils with learning difficulties are frequently referred to other agencies. Health services, such as speech and language therapy, or physiotherapy, occupational therapy, social services, or learning or behaviour support services, may well be involved with the child and his/her family. Incorporate targets from these agencies into a pupil's IEP, and this will help teachers and therapists or support teachers to work together more effectively.

CASE STUDY **Harriet**

A pupil with Autistic Spectrum Disorder may be referred to the speech and language therapy service to develop social communication skills. Harriet is in Year 4 and she has a diagnosis of Asperger Syndrome. In speech and language therapy she has been working on developing her understanding of idioms. In discussion with the therapist, the teacher suggests that work on understanding idioms could be both a part of Harriet's IEP, and the basis of a series of literacy lessons for the whole class.

Holistic IEPs that are written in conjunction with other agencies stand a much greater chance of effectiveness in helping the pupil achieve success. Sharing the responsibility in this way leavens the work of writing and monitoring IEPs. This kind of collaborative working means that SENCOs and teachers should feel less isolated in dealing with the complexities of the SEN Code of Practice. Never dive alone!

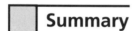

Summary

The P scales are a rich resource for all schools, and provide the small steps to success that support the inclusion of pupils with special educational needs. However, they are only a tool, and it is important to look at the whole child – strengths, talents, interests and special needs – when measuring progress. The P scales are also valuable as a source of targets for individual education plans, showing progression that leads towards and into the National Curriculum.

In short, IEPs should:

- be achievable and realistic;
- meet individual needs;
- have a time frame;
- be agreed with the pupil, parents and other professionals;
- be shared with all staff who work with the student;
- be celebrated when targets are achieved.

Chapter 6 looks at the social interaction and behaviour of pupils with learning difficulties.

Want to play?
Social interaction and behaviour

6

Social interaction

Social interaction with other children is a major reason for including pupils with learning difficulties in mainstream schools. When among other children of the same age pupils gain good models of appropriate play, language and behaviour. Other pupils in the school learn about difference and disability, and become more accepting of diversity in society.

For the families of children with learning difficulties, social interaction and acceptance is a major priority. They want their child to be happy in school, and if that is achieved other more academic concerns become less significant. Parents are just as pleased when their child is invited to a birthday party as they are when they achieve an IEP target.

Led by a teacher or a speech and language therapist, classes in social skills or social use of language will help to develop these skills to some extent. But pupils also need opportunities to try out what they have learned, and to generalise their new skills in different situations. They need the chance to play.

Spiritual, moral, social and cultural development

> . . . a set of values, principles and beliefs . . . to inform their perspective on life and their behaviour. They will defend their beliefs, challenge unfairness and all that would constrain their personal growth, for example, poverty of aspiration, lack of self-confidence and belief, aggression, greed, injustice, narrowness of vision and all forms of discrimination. (Ofsted 2003: 67)

The inclusion of children with more significant special educational needs and disabilities will impact on the spiritual, moral, social and cultural (SMSC) development of all pupils in mainstream schools. Very young children accept without question others who are different or who have a disability, he/she being just another playmate. However, as they move into the later primary years, children begin to take on the values of their families, friends and a wider society. They can become less tolerant of differences, and they may be embarrassed to have a person with a disability as a member of their social group. No school should accept this situation as simply inevitable, because it can be remedied. Every adult who works in the school must model non-discriminatory values and behaviour if stronger, less inclusive, forces from outside school are to be countered. This may mean, for example, adding library books that contain positive images of people with disabilities to balance the negative stereotypes in literature and other media (such as Captain Hook in *Peter Pan*, Rumpelstiltskin, Uncle Craven in *The Secret Garden*, *The Phantom of the Opera*, etc.), or inviting an athlete with a disability to open sports day.

Schools can intervene to help pupils develop social and interaction skills, and to help them maintain their place within a social group. However, equally important are systems which help other pupils become more accepting of diversity. Work in PSHE focusing on relationships fosters and supports these social networks throughout the school by:

- recognising and valuing the worth of each individual;
- developing an ethos in which all pupils can grow and flourish, respect others and be respected;
- accommodating difference and respecting the integrity of individuals.
  (Ofsted 2001)

A buddy system or Circle of Friends (see Chapter 4) provides a framework in which real relationships can develop. It is highly likely that, depending on the individual pupil's changing level of interaction, these systems will need to be used more than once.

Extra-curricular activities

Pupils with learning difficulties may have hidden talents or interests that the school can use to develop interaction, either in lessons or in after-school clubs and activities. A pupil may have an excellent singing voice, a love of painting, be keen on trampolining or interested in computer games. Extra-curricular clubs and activities are a great way to include pupils with learning difficulties in situations that guarantee success and interaction.

Transport issues involving taxis and minibuses are often cited as a barrier to participation in after-school activities. However, these activities are part of the education and associated services offered by a school and children with special educational needs and disabilities have a right to be included in them (DRC 2002). Problems with transport are not insurmountable and parents are often very willing to provide transport themselves if it means their child can join in with extra-curricular activities.

Grouping strategies

It is important for all children to learn to work and play co-operatively. Every day pupils are expected to work in groups of different sizes. Here are some suggestions for grouping pupils that both support the inclusion of children with learning difficulties and enhance the learning experiences for all the class.

- *Pupils work in pairs for part of each lesson, discussing topics or sharing ideas that are then fed back to the whole group.*
  The pupil with learning difficulties may give an interesting new perspective to discussions. Changing the partner each lesson would prevent any one pupil taking on too much of a support role, and may encourage others to develop the caring side of their personality.

- *Create small groups within the classroom which receive additional attention from the teacher or teaching assistant.*
  With this strategy the pupil receives help from both peers and staff. Vary the groups in each lesson so that no one group always includes the pupil with learning difficulties.
- *Create small groups which, with a teacher or teaching assistant, work outside the ordinary classroom for part of the time.*
  This form of withdrawal should be used sparingly as pupils need to become used to working in the classroom environment.
- *Pupil-led groups that discuss an aspect of a lesson and give feedback to the whole class.*
  This tactic gives pupils responsibility for some of their own learning and encourages co-operation. Management of this kind of group can be problematic, especially where some pupils are more dominant than others. A more formal approach may be more appropriate, such as a co-operative learning 'Jigsaw' strategy for groups with a wide spread of abilities.
- *Small-group withdrawal to prepare pupils for inclusion in a later lesson as opposed to withdrawal for parallel teaching.*
  The teacher or teaching assistant helps prepare pupils for work to be covered in a forthcoming lesson. This could include learning facts, preparing questions, or putting together a presentation for the rest of the class.

Co-operative learning

Co-operative learning is a teaching strategy in which small teams, each consisting of pupils with differing levels of ability, use a variety of learning activities to improve their understanding of a subject. Each member of a team is responsible not only for their own learning but also for helping their team-mates to learn, so creating an atmosphere of achievement. Pupils work through an assignment until all the members of the team understand it successfully and it is completed.

Co-operative learning strategies are useful because they reduce peer competition and isolation, and promote academic achievement and positive inter-relationships. The lessons are interactive and the children are expected to listen to each other, ask questions and clarify ideas. Teachers can use peer interactions and other carefully designed activities that help students make connections between concrete and abstract levels of instruction.

Co-operative learning methods share certain characteristics:

- Children work together on common activities that are learned best through team work.
- Pupils work together in small teams of between two and six pupils.
- Pupils use co-operative behaviour to complete learning activities.
- Activities are structured so that pupils have to work together if they are to complete the learning activities.
- Pupils are individually accountable for their own learning.

The elements of co-operative learning are:

- *Positive interdependence*: The efforts of each group member are indispensable if the group is to be successful;
- *Face-to-face interaction*: Teaching the other pupils in the group and checking for understanding;

- *Individual and group accountability*: Each individual team member is accountable for his or her own learning, and for the learning of the others in the team. The group is accountable for supporting their own team members;
- *Interpersonal and small-group skills*: Supports the development of social skills such as leadership, decision-making and communication;
- *Group processing*: Team members discuss how well they achieved their goal and describe what they found useful.

One system of co-operative learning that is relatively simple and which can be used in most subjects is Jigsaw (Aronson and Patnoe 1997).

How to arrange a Jigsaw activity

1. Divide the class into teams of five or six children. In terms of ability the teams should be as diverse as possible.
2. Appoint one pupil from each team to be the leader.
3. Divide the lesson into five or six segments, depending on the number of pupils in the groups. The level of challenge in each segment can be varied to meet the abilities of individual pupils.
4. Assign each pupil one segment to learn. Pupils have access only to their own segment.
5. Give pupils time to read through their segment at least twice. For some pupils the written material will need to have supporting symbols or be available on a personal stereo. There is no need for pupils to memorise the information.
6. Form temporary 'expert' groups by having one pupil from each group join other pupils assigned to the same segment. Give the expert groups time to discuss the main points of their segment, and to devise and rehearse the presentations they will make to their own teams.
7. Regroup pupils back into their original teams.
8. Ask each pupil to present his or her segment to the team. Encourage other pupils in the team to ask questions for clarification.
9. The teacher moves from team to team, observing the process and making any necessary interventions.
10. At the end of the session, give a quiz on the information learned so that pupils realise that they all benefit from learning together.

Box 6.1	Jigsaw in the classroom: Year 5 History

QCA Schemes of Work for history: Unit 11: What was it like for children living in Victorian Britain? (QCA 1998).

One hour lesson. Class of 30 pupils. Class divides into groups of five.

This is the final lesson in the unit. The topic is divided up by the teacher into five segments, each linked to a previous lesson:

- When did the Victorians live?
- What was life like for poor children in Victorian Britain?
- What were Victorian schools like?
- What did Victorian children do in their spare time?
- Who helped to improve the lives of Victorian children?

All the Jigsaw teams have one member assigned to each segment.

The children then divide into 'expert' groups together with the other pupils working on the same segment. These expert groups have access to a variety of information; books from the library, their own history folders, internet sites and videos to enable them to gather information. The expert groups have 20 minutes to collect the necessary information and to decide on the five key points to take back to their Jigsaw teams.

The children return to their Jigsaw teams and each pupil then presents the key points about their segment. Each pupil has five minutes to deliver their information. Other pupils ask questions to clarify points.

The teacher gives the class a quiz on the main points of the topic for the final fifteen

A win-win situation

Including pupils with learning difficulties in mainstream lessons is challenging – but in a positive way. Teachers say that including these pupils often takes them back to the core of their vocation – being creative with the curriculum and identifying the really important aspects of what is taught. Other pupils too will enjoy the challenge of learning in new ways. There is currently a great deal of research into the differing learning styles of pupils. Much of the differentiation we need to make for pupils with learning difficulties involves making learning more visual, and more kinaesthetic. Where teachers strike a balance in their lessons between the auditory, the visual and the kinaesthetic, pupils achieve more and there is a lower incidence of disruptive behaviour.

When all pupils are included and respected in groups within lessons the achievement of all improves. Inclusion is not about educating pupils with learning difficulties at the expense of others. It is about making schools more effective and responsive for all.

The grouping checklist (Figure 6.1) can be used to track a pupil's involvement in different groups over several weeks. It offers teachers and teaching assistants a method of gauging the level of formal and informal interactions with which a student is engaged. This information will be valuable when reporting to annual reviews and when preparing individual education plans. The checklist might be used to inform individual lesson planning as well as longer term plans. A blank version of the checklist is included on the CD (Figure 6.2).

Behaviour

A pupil with learning difficulties very rarely has behaviour difficulties attributable directly to his/her learning disability. When pupils are offered appropriate activities at which they can succeed, behaviour difficulties will be kept to a minimum. As with all pupils, those with learning difficulties will behave better in situations where they feel confident and valued. When they are given work that

Name: Siân **Class/Year group:** 2 MJ **Lesson:** Literacy **Teacher:** Miss Jarvis

Date	1/11	2/11	3/11	4/11	5/11	8/11	9/11	10/11	11/11	12/11
Whole class involvement	5 minutes	10 minutes		10 minutes	10 minutes	10 minutes	15 minutes		5 minutes	6 minutes
Group work										
In class		✓		✓	✓	✓	✓			✓
Withdrawal	✓		✓					✓		
TA support	✓		✓			✓		✓		✓
Peer support		✓		✓	✓		✓			
Pairs										
With TA	✓			✓	✓	✓	✓		✓	
With peer		✓								
Informal interactions	Sang Happy Birthday to Jade	Phonics worksheet with Bethan	in SrLT room	giggling with Jade in line	Chosen to sit away from MSP in assembly	Asked to borrow Ali's rubber	worked on computer with Jade	speech therapy	1-1 with Mrs Peter (unwell)	told school about her Dad's marathon during assembly

FIGURE 6.1 Completed grouping checklist

is too complex – or too easy – behaviour will deteriorate. Challenging behaviour is almost always the pupils' response to the demands made on them, or to something in the school environment. It is not necessarily an inherent problem within the pupil, or related to their disability (Jones 2002), but rather an indicator of how the pupil feels in a particular situation. Find out what is triggering the behaviour, and ask parents if they have noticed any changes at home.

Any sudden deterioration in behaviour always signals a change of some kind. It could be the onset of illness or pain, a reaction to a change in the usual environment – such as a new pupil in the class or a supply teacher – or anxiety about a situation at home or in the playground. Take time to try to find out what change has triggered the behaviour and identify how the pupil may be supported through this difficult period.

In Alfie's case the behaviour may be the child's way of communicating his feelings about a difficult situation:

CASE STUDY **Alfie**

Alfie is in Year 2. He has Prader-Willi Syndrome and moderate learning difficulties. He is a friendly child who has never exhibited any behaviour problems. The syndrome causes Alfie to be hungry all the time and he is significantly overweight. Over a period of a few weeks Alfie became increasingly reluctant to come into school in the mornings, and took almost an hour to eat his dinner. When he was told to go outside or eat more quickly he became angry and aggressive to the point of biting a teaching assistant's hand. His parents were called in and told that if his aggressive behaviour continued for much longer, the school would seek to have Alfie moved to a special school.

Fortunately for Alfie, a teacher on playground duty spotted him crying and shaking with fear across the playground on the periphery of a group of boys playing football. The teacher led Alfie away and asked him why he was crying. He said was frightened of the football game which ranged across the playground before school and in the dinner break. To adjust the situation the school set up small goalposts on one side of the playground to keep the football within a restricted area, and sited a couple of wooden benches close to the school buildings. Gradually Alfie overcame his fear of the football game and happily sat on a bench and his behaviour returned to normal.

Continual anxiety or stress has a significant impact on behaviour for adults as well as children, and wherever possible schools should look to remove any source of that anxiety. Imagine you have a fear of heights but every day you are forced to go to the very top of Blackpool Tower – and stay there for many hours. You try to communicate how you feel to the people forcing you to do this, but still they make you go up there. How would you feel? How will you behave?

After a period of time you might accept that you had to go up the tower every day, but you would still experience a high level of anxiety. You would worry about it at night and your sleep patterns would be disrupted. You would spend much of every day suppressing the urge to escape from that situation. You would become irritable and withdrawn and feel angry and resentful towards the people causing you this anxiety. Does this sound familiar?

For some children, especially those with Autistic Spectrum Disorder, this anxiety is a constant burden. Indeed it has been likened to the level of stress that we feel just before a job interview. How difficult must it be to have to do school work in addition to dealing with this anxiety? Sometimes just a change of teacher, TA or classroom can bring about huge improvements in behaviour. There may be something about a particular person or place that upsets the child at a fundamental level. The child may not be able to articulate his/her feelings, but they are no less real for all that.

Responses such as sending them to stand outside the room, shouting or exhortations to 'be good' will not be effective ways of dealing with children with learning difficulties. It is important to look for the reason behind the behaviour, and if possible address the cause of the problem. Observe the pupil in different lessons and at various times of the day. It is possible the child is 'playing to the gallery', getting attention from other pupils by behaving inappropriately, or perhaps he/she is copying behaviour seen on the playground or at home.

ABC

The best way of discovering why pupils use inappropriate behaviour is to observe them and identify 'flashpoints' – times in the school day when their behaviour becomes less appropriate. An ABC (Antecedents, Behaviours and Consequences) assessment of situations can be undertaken, preferably by a colleague who does not currently teach the pupil. In this way the process remains relatively dispassionate. This assessment should give a clearer understanding of the behaviours, and provide clues as to how to move forward.

Antecedents
Identify what has led to the inappropriate behaviour. For example:

- Does the behaviour happen before or during some lessons more than others?
- Are particular pupils regularly involved?
- Could there be any sensory reasons for the behaviour (such as the noise of computers or a flickering fluorescent light)?

Behaviour
Describe the exact nature of the inappropriate behaviour.

- Be precise when describing behaviour as differences may reflect differing reasons. For example, running out of class may be because the pupil is anxious or afraid, whereas running around the room may be to gain an adult's attention.

Consequences
Describe what happened as a consequence of the behaviour.

- How did the pupil react?
- How did other pupils react?
- How did the adults in the room react?
- Was the pupil punished? If so, how?
- Did the pupil receive the pay-off he or she wanted?
- Were there any longer-term consequences, such as parents being informed?

An ABC observation form (Figure 6.3) can be found on the facing page.

ABC Record	Name:	Class/Year group:	Date:

Pupil's strengths and interests:

Antecedents: what happens before the behaviours?	**Behaviours:** describe the behaviours
What is the pupil trying to communicate?	**Consequences:** what happens after the behaviours?
	What prevention strategies are in place?
	What alternative behaviours are being taught?

FIGURE 6.3   ABC behaviour observation form

Children who constantly seek attention

Both at home and in school all children crave attention from adults. Most children learn that if they work hard and behave well they will receive positive attention from their teacher. Other children learn that the only way to get the attention they need is to misbehave, for then they get plenty of attention – negative attention – but attention nonetheless. This can be a deliberate ploy by the more able children, but with children who have learning difficulties it is likely to be a learned response that has been reinforced over time.

Accentuate the positive

Wherever possible praise anything the child does that is positive. This does take time to work, but will have the desired effect in the end. Minimise the language used when giving praise, so that the pupil knows exactly what behaviour you want. Phrases such as 'Good listening', 'I like the way you waited for us', or 'Thank you for putting your book away', are perfect when said with a smile. Pupils eventually learn which behaviours are acceptable and which are not. This 'shower of affirmation' approach is very powerful and will transform a child's behaviour, but can be galling to do, especially if the pupil has a long history of challenging behaviour. Just give it time, and you will see the dividends in terms of less disruption in the class and less stress for the staff.

It is worth trying always to accentuate the positive, because the alternative is the 'he/she mustn't get away with it' approach, with a stream of corrections and reprimands. Reprimands quickly lose effect when pupils constantly are being told off and, although it is negative, getting the attention they crave. The situation then escalates with pupils becoming increasingly a nuisance in class and needing increasingly severe sanctions. This situation is in no-one's interest, serves only to make teachers and teaching assistants stressed, and makes the pupil with learning difficulties unhappy and confused.

The other side of accentuating the positive is even harder – playing down the negative. Being good rarely leads to adults giving children the attention they crave. On the other hand, inappropriate behaviour is guaranteed to get a response – it rings the bell every time – and ensures a predictable response from adults. The more extreme the behaviour, the more certain is the adult's reaction. When the child is behaving inappropriately pay him/her absolutely no attention – no eye-contact, not even 'the look'. This will clearly demonstrate that such behaviour will not win the required attention. To ignore inappropriate behaviour really goes against the grain for teachers and teaching assistants. They feel that if they ignore the behaviour, the pupil is 'getting away with it' and that it is unfair to other pupils. But ignoring some behaviours does work – eventually. Other pupils (without feeling that they have to try it too) usually are sufficiently aware to understand that teachers are trying to help the child behave more appropriately.

The 'boomerang effect'

Another strategy to help children who crave constant attention is the 'boomerang effect'. Give the child positive attention in some form – a word of praise, a smile, a hand on the shoulder – every five minutes throughout the lesson. You can put a sand timer on the table and tell the child, 'I'll be back when the sand runs out'. Do not return until the sand has run through, no matter how much fuss the child makes. Again, give positive attention for a few seconds, reset the timer, and move away. After a couple of days, set the timer to last ten minutes and repeat the process. This strategy teaches the pupil that he/she will get attention but at the time set by the adult, rather than according to the child's agenda. It takes time and a lot of effort to re-educate the child, but it is worth it when the challenging behaviour diminishes.

It is very stressful to have a child with challenging behaviour in the classroom. The stress is cumulative, and gradually erodes good will and the determination to include. It feels personal, and quickly can become a vicious cycle of unacceptable behaviour from the child, and anger and frustration from the adults; but the likelihood is that both the adult and the child in the situation are angry and frustrated. Those feelings need to be diffused – at least on one side – if improvements are to be made.

Here are a few steps teachers and TAs can take to bring about those improvements:

A new beginning every day

Make each morning a fresh start. Greet the child with a smile and a cheery hello and tell him/her what exciting activities are planned for the day. Pupils with learning difficulties may remember little of what went on the previous day, and even if they do remember, may not understand how their behaviour caused the problem. Feelings that are allowed to hangover from previous days will only add to stress on both sides. If the same problem is occurring frequently, think about using a social story to help the child understand how his or her behaviour is inappropriate.

Talk to parents

Let parents know when there is a problem before it escalates into a crisis. A direct contact by phone or home visit means the problem is shared and can be addressed in both settings.

Listen to parents

Sometimes children behave very differently at home from in school; they can be very good in school and difficult at home, and vice-versa. No parent wants their child to be in trouble at school, and a close relationship between teacher and parents produces a formidable team with which to address the inappropriate behaviour.

Take out the personal

Keep a professional distance between the child's behaviour and your own feelings. Children with learning difficulties do not have the sophistication or guile to set out deliberately to wind up their teacher. Their behaviour is either a response to something which causes them distress in the classroom environment, or they have learned that the behaviour wins them the attention they seek. By staying emotionally neutral, the teacher or teaching assistant is the better able to judge the situation and to respond appropriately. The child may have learning difficulties, but first and foremost he/she is just a child. Stay 'in the adult' and take out personal feelings; the stress will be reduced and it will be possible to take a more objective view of the behaviours.

Teach!

This may seem a strange recommendation, but it is surprising how often a teacher complains about how a child behaves, yet has not tried to teach the child an alternative, more appropriate way of dealing with a situation. Make your requirements explicit to the pupil. Let the pupil know exactly how you expect them to behave and what they *should* do in the situation.

For example, every time a girl in Year 1 goes into the hall for assembly, she talks loudly to the teacher or to another child, she calls out to the head teacher when he is addressing the school, and frequently gets up and wanders out to the toilet. Why does she behave like this?

1. She hasn't learned that one has to vary vocal tone and pitch according to situation. It is appropriate to speak loudly in the playground, maybe at home, but not in assembly.
2. She does not understand that when the head teacher is addressing the whole school he is not directing his speech at her, and so she responds just as she does when her mum speaks to her at home.
3. At home, she is allowed to go to the toilet when she needs to. She does not understand yet that before she goes to the toilet at school she should ask first, or wait until a particular time.

At first the social norms of school, such as waiting in line or asking permission before going to the toilet, will not be understood by pupils with learning difficulties. These norms will need to be explicitly taught. Strategies such as social stories (Gray 1994a) will help the child to learn behaviours that are appropriate for particular school situations.

Behaviour prompt cards

Behaviour prompt pictures/symbols are an effective way to remind pupils of how they should behave in class. Symbols such as 'be quiet', 'wait', or 'sit down', can be held towards the pupil by the teacher or teaching assistant. This method is particularly useful where a teaching assistant is observing and supporting the whole class. The prompts can be used for any pupil who needs a reminder, and the cards do not necessarily require any additional comment or action. If symbols are used the pupils would need to learn their meanings, but they would then be useful for all children, including those with literacy difficulties.

Should a pupil's behaviour become either too dangerous or too disruptive some action has to be taken. The most effective course of action is to divert the pupil's attention away from the inappropriate behaviour and onto a more positive activity. With young children, point to something across the room or move them to a different area. This will often refocus their attention and restore calm.

The child can be given a task to distract them. Cleaning the whiteboard, taking the register to the office, or a note to the secretary, will each build up self-esteem. The pupil also has a break of concentration and has a little physical exercise. Most pupils promptly forget any previous difficulties and settle back to work. A teaching assistant could shadow the pupil from a distance should there be concerns about the child's safety outside the classroom. Dealing with disruptive behaviour in this way causes minimal disruption for the teacher, the class,

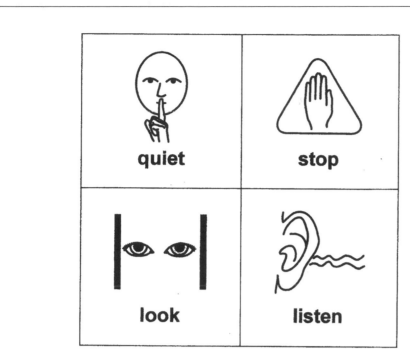

FIGURE 6.4   Behaviour prompt cards

and the individual pupil. Anger management techniques may be appropriate for use with older pupils, and information and advice on this can be sought from your LEA behaviour support team.

Inevitably there will be occasions when behaviour goes beyond low-level aggravation and some form of verbal chastisement is necessary. The correction should take place immediately, but in any case as soon as possible after the incident has occurred. If you wait until the end of the lesson, or even the end of the day, the pupil will have forgotten what happened and will not understand why they are being chastised.

Simple language and short phrases immediately expressed are very effective. When angry our vocal tone rises, we speak more quickly and use more complex words, sentences, and structures including irony and sarcasm. Pupils who have comprehension difficulties (and that includes almost all children with learning difficulties) will not understand what is being said. These pupils will actively switch off, with the speech becoming simply a wash of sound.

Use a form of words that condemns the inappropriate behaviour rather than the child, such as, 'Don't call out. If you want to speak, put your hand up.' Being told that they are 'naughty' or 'bad' does not help pupils to change behaviours and can seriously damage self-esteem, confidence and motivation. Tell the pupil what they did that was wrong, and then tell them what they should have done – when they know how to behave there is a greater likelihood of future compliance.

Rules

The majority of children with learning difficulties will obey school rules, but only when they know and understand them. They will need opportunities to learn the school rules, and time to talk about them with an adult. Only when this has been done can pupils with learning difficulties be expected to know and obey school rules. Some pupils need to have additional, individual rules that will help them manage their own behaviour in situations they find difficult. A pupil with learning difficulties may not know such things as:

- you have to keep quiet when the teacher is talking;
- you mustn't climb on the wall outside;
- you eat your snack at play time;
- you ask before going to the toilet.

A few specific personal rules can be written on card and laminated. A child with reading difficulties could have the rules in the form of pictures or symbols. The pupil's parents will need to have a copy, and the rules can be shared at home as well as with the teacher or a teaching assistant at the start of each day. Individual rules frequently deflect potential problems and misunderstandings, and they take little time and effort to put in place.

Offer practical alternatives when unacceptable behaviour is repeated. For example, when a pupil has to line up all her pens and pencils on the desk before starting work, try providing her with a desk tidy or a see-through pencil case. Such a simple action often can defuse a potentially explosive situation.

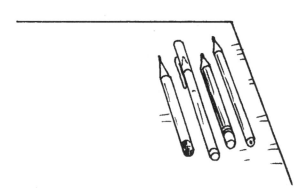

One step at a time

Where a pupil uses several unacceptable behaviours in school, try to change only one behaviour at a time. Talk with the pupil about the behaviour that needs to change, and teach an acceptable alternative. Make regular notes on the changes in the pupil's behaviour. This may seem like excessive record keeping, but when teachers and teaching assistants see the behaviour improving, they begin to feel better about both themselves and the pupil! If the changes are not written down it can be easy to miss these improvements. They must be celebrated with the pupil, with their parents, and amongst the staff. To change staff perceptions of a pupil is often as important as changing the pupil's behaviour. 'Once a nuisance always a nuisance' attitudes can persist – even when the pupil's behaviour has improved dramatically.

Whole-staff understanding

Where there are adults in the school who do not understand the reasons for a pupil's behaviour, a negative or angry response from just one adult can cause the child great distress. Pupils with learning difficulties will often have no behaviour difficulties in class, but may experience conflicts with other pupils at dinner or play times. To manage such situations requires a high level of understanding and skill. Lunchtime supervisors, administrators or cleaning staff rarely have training in behaviour management and usually have to rely on their own experiences of school or of raising children. Inappropriate management can turn minor arguments into major incidents.

Allocate time at the start of each school year to pass on information to all staff about particular children with learning or behavioural difficulties, a little time spent in this way may well avoid future difficulties.

Equal and realistic expectations

Make sure teachers and teaching assistants have realistic expectations of how a pupil with learning difficulties should and could behave. Each child has their own personality traits and quirks which may annoy others. Some pupils have physical tics that they cannot control. Some pupils hum quietly – or not so quietly – when they are concentrating; others may make noises intermittently or have stereotypical behaviours, such as turning around before they sit down. These individual traits need to be taken into account before a pupil's behaviour can be described as disruptive.

Pupils with learning difficulties are monitored closely throughout the day, much more so than other pupils, and teachers and teaching assistants make sure they stay on task throughout lessons. If you observe other pupils *without* learning difficulties, you find that they attend intermittently; sometimes listening or working, other times looking out of the window or chatting to a friend. Be sure not to demand higher standards of behaviour from pupils with learning difficulties than you expect from other children. A valuable way of evaluating how well a pupil is performing in lessons is observation by colleagues. Monitoring the time that all pupils stay on task will give an accurate picture of how hard the pupil with learning difficulties is working in comparison to others.

Can't or won't

It can be very difficult to determine when a pupil is unable to do work or when he/she is simply refusing to try. Teachers gauge a reason for a lack of work from what the pupils say, how they say it, from eye-contact, from facial expression, and from body language. All this information, combined with previous knowledge of the pupil's work, determines the teacher's response. Is the pupil to be given extra help, or made to stay in at play time?

'Can't or won't' is less straightforward with children with learning difficulties. They may appear to be refusing to attempt the work, or to be taking an inordinately long time. It may be impossible for the pupil to say why the work has not been completed. He/she may seem not to be bothered about the lack of work, or may appear defiant. However, an apparent attitude or facial expression can be misleading as the child, especially when still quite young, will not have the sophistication deliberately to transmit such complex feelings. The most likely explanation is that the work is a little too difficult – so change the task for something within the child's capability.

'Manipiulative' pupils?

Frequently teachers report that pupils with learning difficulties are 'manipulative'. With more careful questioning this is found to mean that the pupil wants to get their own way. No different from other children then! As they grow, all children eventually learn that they have to wait for things or conform to requests. Children still want their own way, but most also want to please adults. Pupils with learning difficulties take longer to learn this particular social skill. They may not necessarily want to please a particular adult, and are likely only to have access to more immature strategies. To deliberately manipulate an adult into behaving in a certain way a child has to have some understanding of how adults think and of adult motivations. This is a level of sophistication beyond the developmental level of children with learning difficulties in the primary phase.

Tiredness

In order to understand and respond to lessons in school, children with learning difficulties have to work very hard. The effort they expend will be greater than almost any other pupil in the class. Once most other pupils learn a routine they need hardly to think about it, whereas pupils with learning difficulties need to think about almost everything, every time. They can take little for granted. This is another reason why visual cues and lists are so useful. Pupils with learning difficulties need to remember and think actively about such things as how to write their name, the equipment they will need for each activity, and changing for swimming. This constant active thinking in addition to the school work and the effort of social interaction causes pupils with learning difficulties to become very tired by the end of the school day.

The impact of illness on behaviour

As with all pupils, the behaviour of pupils with learning difficulties will change when they are ill. Unfortunately it is not possible to anticipate how a child's behaviour will change. Some pupils become very withdrawn and quiet, others have an opposite reaction. Try to find out if illness could be the cause of negative changes in a pupil's behaviour. Often a telephone call to parents will answer concerns before a difficult situation develops in school.

The following case study is not to condone Jake's behaviour, but to explain why the incidents occurred.

Jake

Jake in Year 6 has severe learning difficulties. He usually behaves well in school, but he is sometimes wilful and can refuse to do as he is asked.

At the start of the spring term Jake's behaviour deteriorated rapidly. He became increasingly resistant to requests to work, and was verbally and physically abusive to the teachers, teaching assistants, and other pupils. Jake's behaviour was also very challenging at home, especially as he no longer slept through the night. He appeared unhappy and anxious. In the week before half term Jake kicked and injured a teacher's leg. In line with school policy Jake was given a temporary exclusion, and several teachers and parents lobbied the governors to have him permanently removed from the school.

Jake's parents were very concerned and so took him to see the family doctor. The doctor discovered that Jake had a very serious ear infection that would have caused him continual discomfort. He was given antibiotics and after a few days his behaviour returned to normal.

Jake did not have the language skills to express the pain he was experiencing. His only way of showing the distress was through his behaviour.

Medication

Some children with learning difficulties need to take medicines for conditions such as epilepsy. It may take several months for doctors to perfect the choice and dosage of medication for a particular individual, and the pupil's behaviour is likely to be erratic during this time. Communication with parents is obviously of vital importance in this situation, and school staff will need to be understanding and more tolerant than normal of unusual behaviour.

Unstructured time in school

Most pupils with learning difficulties quickly learn how to behave appropriately in lessons. They become familiar and comfortable in the structured settings and behave accordingly. Problems frequently arise in less structured times in school, such as any transitions between lessons, moving into the hall, dinner and play times. Problems often arise because of misunderstandings between pupils, or because the child with learning difficulties does not know what they are expected to do and how they should behave. A buddy system or Circle of Friends (see Chapter 4) can give support during play times. An invitation to join games from a member of a Circle of Friends will often make the world of difference to a pupil's behaviour and confidence.

Teaching assistants need to be deployed with sensitivity during dinner times and play times. Rather than assigning an adult to accompany a child, encourage a 'watching brief' where the child is observed from a distance. An adult trailing round, especially if holding the child's hand, serves only to make the pupil appear more different to others, and makes interaction much less likely. Some head teachers refer to one-to-one teaching assistants as 'minders' and sometimes it is easy to see why.

Some schools have introduced playground games, especially for younger children. Group games, such as 'What's the time, Mr Wolf' or 'In and Out the Windows', are ideal for involving all children together as they require no special skills, and they are great fun.

The vocabulary of feelings

In order to effect changes in our behaviour we need to be able to think about and understand why we behave in certain ways. Underpinning understanding is the rich vocabulary of words relating to emotions. We have access to a wonderfully rich and complex language through which we express and consider our feelings in precise detail. Children with learning difficulties will develop this emotional vocabulary much later than their peers, and this can deny them the ability fully to reflect and think through the reasons for their own behaviours.

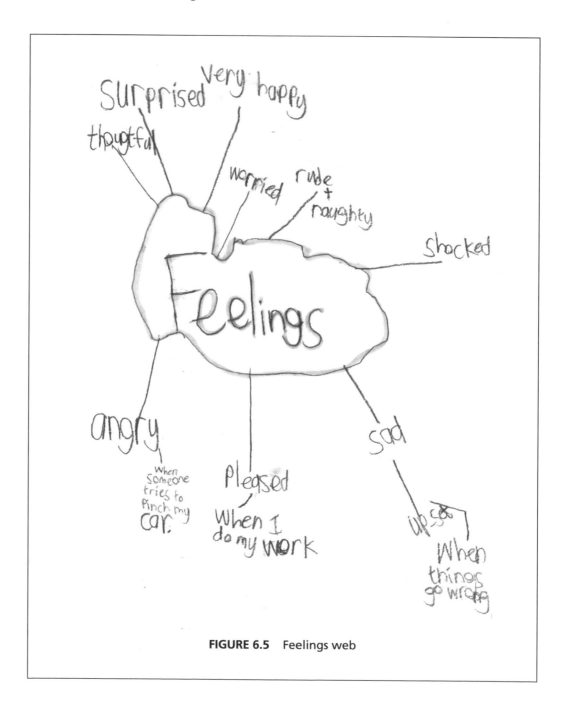

FIGURE 6.5   Feelings web

Teachers need to build opportunities into the curriculum for children to develop and reinforce a vocabulary of feelings. The opportunities could form part of the PSHE programme or be woven into lessons across the curriculum. Examples are:

- a discussion about how a story character feels in literacy;
- exploring the colours of emotions in art; or
- creating mood effects in music.

Linked to this limited vocabulary of feelings is the child's incomplete understanding of the impact of their own behaviour on other people's feelings. This may be due to immaturity, with acting out being the child's only release for frustration, or it could be a lack of empathy which may persist into adulthood. Either way the adults who work with a child with learning difficulties must avoid taking challenging behaviour personally, or being hurt and upset by it. It isn't aimed at you – you just happened to be in the way!

Social stories

This approach is based on the social stories method devised by Carol Gray (1994a). Social stories are written by an adult who knows the pupil well, such as a teacher, parent or teaching assistant. The story helps the child to understand the situations they find difficult and lets the pupil know what to expect and how to behave. A social story should be short, and may include photographs, drawings and/or symbols. The story needs to give the pupil information about where and when the situation occurs, who is involved, what usually happens and why (Jones 2002). Sometimes reading just two or three sentences regularly with the pupil can prompt changes in understanding and behaviour. Harry in Year 1, whose social story is below, responds to the bell at the end of playtime by running away. The teacher or teaching assistant tries to catch him, but he is very quick and has to be coaxed back inside, which can take a long time.

CASE STUDY **Harry's social story**

At play times we go outside to the playground. If it is raining we go into the hall to play. We can run or play games. At the end of play, the teacher rings the bell. The first ring means we have to stand still. Standing still means not walking or running and staying in the same place. On the second ring we walk into school. When we get into school we can have a drink and our snack.

Summary

Inappropriate or challenging behaviour is the major reason for the breakdown in placements in mainstream schools for children with learning difficulties. Yet the source of the problem rarely lies with the pupil, or within the child's learning difficulties. Most behaviour problems are the child's response to something that happens at home or in school. The usual systems of rewards and sanctions may not work with these children, and we need to find new, more creative – perhaps more sensitive – resolutions. By taking time to observe and talk to the child, teachers can discover the underlying reasons for the behaviour, and develop relatively simple and practical solutions.

Chapter 7 gives ideas for communicating with children with learning difficulties and hearing the voice of the child.

Communicating with children who have learning difficulties

This chapter offers strategies that teachers and TAs can use to develop communication with and between pupils. As communication is the basis of interaction between people, a breakdown in communication will have a profound emotional impact on a child. When children are very young, adults support communication by naturally:

- using simple language;
- playing interaction games, such as 'This little piggy';
- encouraging a child's communication with smiles and eye contact;
- reinforcing language with repetition;
- valuing all attempts at communication.

By contrast, children in Key Stage 2 are expected to communicate almost at an adult level, and when they are unable to – as with a child with a language disorder or a learning difficulty – isolation is the reality every day.

Teachers and other adults in school can be anxious about how to communicate with children with learning difficulties. The children may not have the full range of communication strategies, and so adults will have to try a little harder both to understand what the child has to say and to make themselves understood. But it is so worth taking the trouble to overcome that initial reluctance.

Speech is only one medium of communication. As little as seven per cent of our understanding of language comes from the words we hear. The bulk of the meaning comes from the context of a situation, facial expression, eye gaze, gesture and body language. As communication is about so much more than speech it is essential to maximise other paths to understanding and expression for pupils with communication difficulties.

A useful starting point is to ask someone who knows the pupil well to help you communicate. Parents are best placed to give this help, as they will have developed communication with their child over several years. When a pupil can communicate by speech but has articulation difficulties, you will find that gradually you tune in to their way of speaking. For pupils who need to use signing or a communication aid, however, it can take longer to establish full communication, and some general training will need to be given to all school staff. More specific training should be provided for key adults who will be working with the pupil.

Here are some helpful tips for developing communication with a pupil with learning difficulties:

- When you want to tell the pupil something, or ask them a question, say their name first and then leave a short pause of a second or two. For example, 'Jaime, . . . get me your reading book, please.' This gains the pupil's attention, lets them know that they need to listen, and will give them time to transfer their attention.

- When you ask the pupil a question, allow time to process the question and then for him/her to formulate the answer. A slow count of ten is usually about the right length of time.

- If you think a pupil has not understood, try not to rephrase the question too soon. It will be interpreted as a separate question and will cause confusion.

- Use simple straightforward language in short sentences. This doesn't mean talking down to pupils, but more direct information will help them understand what you want.

- Give validity and respect to pupils' opinions. Show that you value their contributions by repeating what he/she has said, and by your smiling and nodding. This has an added benefit of giving a model of positive communicative behaviour that other children can copy.

- Most pupils with learning difficulties are much stronger visually than aurally. Use objects, photographs, pictures or symbols to support speech. These supports will get the message across much more easily.

- When meeting a pupil for the first time use minimum eye contact. Some pupils find eye contact threatening; this is especially so for those pupils with Autistic Spectrum Disorder.

- If a pupil is trying to tell you something and you do not understand, ask him/her to repeat what they have said. If you still do not understand, say so, but ask the child to tell someone they know well who might be more 'tuned in'. Look around for clues, and ask the pupil to point to or draw something which might help.

- Try not to finish off pupils' sentences, even if you think you know what they are going to say. It is annoying, and you will probably be wrong. By all means smile and encourage them to keep trying, but if they think they don't need to try to communicate they won't bother next time!

Communicative intent

From the very earliest days of life children communicate with their significant adults. That first communication is through crying and squirming and has the function of conveying hunger or distress. As the baby grows this communication develops into eye contact, smiles and gurgles, and adults respond with more smiles, soft touches and words, all of which reinforce the desire to communicate. However, for some children that desire or *intent* to communicate is incomplete to some degree. This could be because of early experiences due to illness or a sensory impairment, or it could be linked to Autistic Spectrum Disorder. For these children an understanding of the function of communication will be developed through linking speech, signs or symbols, with activities and objects that motivate and enthuse the child.

There are many different modes of communication that people use either on their own, or in combinations:

Vocalisation

When pupils have limited or no speech they may use other vocal sounds to attempt to communicate, as in the case study below about Catherine, who desperately wanted to make herself understood and used the sound 'h' for hat in conjunction with gesture. If adults or other children ignore or laugh at these vocalisations, the child's self-confidence will gradually be eroded and he/she will stop trying.

Facial expression

Facial expression is probably, after speech, the most effective form of communication, although it requires a relatively high level of sophistication to understand all the possible nuances. Muscle movements that are used to change meaning are very subtle, for instance the difference between a smile and a sneer, but pupils with learning difficulties often use a limited range of expressions. It is also worth remembering that facial expression does not always reflect what a person with learning difficulties is thinking. A child may have an 'insolent' expression or smile when being told off. This doesn't necessarily mean the child doesn't care, or that he/she is being rude, but that the understanding is not present to match the facial expression to a range of situations. Pupils with Autistic Spectrum Disorder will have difficulties, both in understanding facial expression and in using it effectively as part of communication.

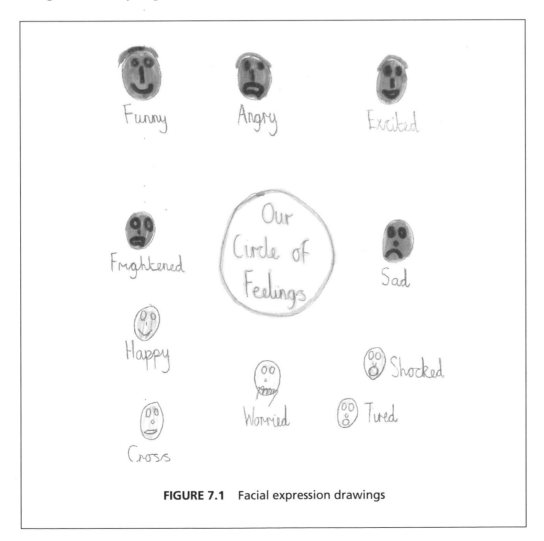

FIGURE 7.1   Facial expression drawings

Physical movement

When all else fails, often pupils will take an adult by the hand to show them what they want. Pupils with Autistic Spectrum Disorder often use this mode of communication. Frequent rocking or pacing is often a sign of distress which should never be ignored, as this may be the child's only way of communicating anxiety or unhappiness.

Gesture

Some pupils who have little or no speech will compensate by using more gesture, but this can be very idiosyncratic and it will take some time to begin to know what the pupil means. In particular, pointing is an important gesture. This needs to be encouraged as it means the child wants to share attention with another person. The pointing means, 'Hey, look at that!' and for some children it can be the first stage of two-way communication.

CASE STUDY **Catherine**

Catherine has a severe communication disorder and communicates using gestures and some Signalong signs. On a hot day in the summer she approached a teaching assistant on duty in the playground. She was clearly distressed, tapping her head with the flat of her hand and making h..h..h . . . sounds. The teaching assistant had had no signing training and so did not attempt to understand what Catherine was communicating. One of Catherine's classmates then came over and told the teaching assistant that Catherine wanted her hat because she was very hot.

In this situation the signing was a red herring and caused the teaching assistant not to respond to Catherine's attempt to communicate. Catherine was distressed and simply wanted to let the adult know that she needed her hat. She used natural gesture and the initial sound which she knew.

Signing

The use of signing is an effective way to support communication for people with learning difficulties. It adds a visual component to speech and formalises the use of gesture. Pupils with learning difficulties should not be expected to sign every word. They can be taught key signs that support their communication at whatever level that may be. Some pupils will use only a few signs that are really important to them, while others may use a large number of signs which support a developing understanding and a complexity of language. Be aware that too much signing may be just as confusing for a child with learning difficulties as can be speech. Sign only those key words which will support the child's understanding, and teach any new signs *before* the child is expected to understand or use them.

Two of the more commonly used signing systems are Signalong and Makaton. Both these systems are a form of sign-supported English based on British Sign Language. They are used in addition to speech, and follow the word order of spoken English. To develop literacy it is possible to link signing to the use of symbols.

Signing can be effective only where a sufficient number of people in the school, both staff and pupils, know some signs. Hiring a trainer for an in-service training session will give the staff basic understanding of the system, and will teach them how to read the manuals. Some schools set up signing clubs at lunchtimes or after school: these clubs teach many pupils this valuable skill which supports and develops children's communication with pupils with learning difficulties.

Body language

Body language is a very powerful and sophisticated communication tool. Posture and movement as we stand or sit, how near or far away we stand from a person – all can change the meaning of what we say. In conversation we often mirror the stance of the person we are talking to, leaning towards someone we like, or crossing our arms when we feel defensive. Pupils with learning difficulties often do not understand other people's body language, and rely too much on the words used. They rarely use body language appropriately and this limits full communication. Adults may need to adapt or explain their body language, and, to help pupils understand, should do so consistently. For instance, crossed arms and foot tapping may tell most children that an adult is cross, but a child with learning difficulties will not pick up on these cues and will need to be told, 'I am angry because . . .' Some children can be taught how to use body language, but rarely does it become a natural skill.

Eye contact

Eye contact is an instinctive and natural element of communication. It lets other people know that we are interested in what they have to say, and is a part of how we extract meaning from language. In many people with learning difficulties the use of eye contact can be a strength, but for others it will be a skill gained only through direct teaching. Where a pupil has been taught how to use eye contact it is rare for him/her to use it entirely naturally. This is particularly true of pupils with Autistic Spectrum Disorder who may find eye contact threatening, or who can be listening intently to what is being said even though they may be looking in the opposite direction. This is a case where getting to know a child, and knowing how they communicate, is of paramount importance.

Objects of reference

The term *objects of reference* is used to describe the use of objects as a means of communication, objects used to represent categories of events and things. For pupils with learning difficulties who may not be able to use or respond to signs, symbols or photographs they are cues to support understanding and communication. The benefit of using objects is that they can be felt, mouthed, smelled, even cuddled. These added dimensions give objects an invaluable role in providing the basis for communication.

Objects of reference can be used in a number of ways:

- as a route to more complex forms of communication, such as symbols or signing;
- to give pupils greater understanding of what is happening around them in the classroom;
- to help pupils *see* a sequence of activities for a lesson or a timetable;
- to give pupils opportunities to make choices and communicate their needs and wants.

Objects of reference can be used in a variety of ways:

Real-life objects

Real-life objects tell the child what is going to happen next, or what is expected of them, such as giving a pupil a pencil at the start of each English lesson, a Unifix cube for a maths lesson, or a pad when it is time to go to the toilet.

Objects on card

The mounting of real life objects onto card provides a link into the use of photographs and symbols. An object on the card is used to represent a particular activity or lesson, and gradually a photograph or symbol is introduced at the same time. In time the object is withdrawn, and only the 2D representation is used.

Miniature objects

Miniature objects are used as the next step where a child has developed some understanding of representation, but still needs the tactile dimension of an object. Dolls house furniture and equipment are very useful for this, and can be relatively inexpensive. A toy fork may be used to represent lunch time, or a toy chair for when a child is expected to sit down to work. A word of warning here however: avoid the use of miniature objects when children are still at the stage of putting objects into their mouth. A real danger for children with learning difficulties is the possibility of their choking on small objects they put into their mouths.

Abstract objects

As pupils become more familiar with the use of objects of reference, the objects can become more abstract with less of a direct link with the activity. For instance, when using a sea shell as the object of reference for science lessons, the important factor is the association built up over time between the activity and the object.

Object timetables

Objects can be used to create an object timetable. The pupil removes the appropriate object at the start of the lesson and keeps it with him/her until the end. This gives a clear *sequence* of activities and tells the pupil *how many* activities before play or home time.

Making choices

Objects of reference enable children to make choices for themselves. It is this ability to communicate preferences and desires that is a major motivating factor for many children. A glove and a piece of puzzle kept in a box by the classroom door can give a child the options, 'Do you want to go outside today or stay in?'

The key to the successful use of objects of reference is to make them:

■ Meaningful: Does the child understand what the adult intends the object to represent?
■ Motivating: A prime reason for communicating is to share information with others. Start with objects linked to activities that the child really enjoys.
■ Frequent: A child with learning difficulties will need to use the objects of reference at least daily if the associations with the activities are to be maintained. Do not expect a child to understand an object of reference that has not been used regularly or recently. (Park 2003)

Begin with one or two objects and frequently occurring situations that the child enjoys. Some children take a little while to start making the associations, but it is always worth persevering with objects of reference because they are a bridge to other forms of communication.

Communication boards and books

Communication boards may be made up of photographs, symbols, or words that are familiar to the child. A communication board can have several functions:

■ to enable the child to initiate interactions;
■ to enable the child to make choices;
■ to give the child opportunities to answer questions;
■ to help the child pass on information to adults or other children;
■ to give adults or other children a way of clarifying information or interacting.

Communication boards can be quite complex depending on the individual child's understanding, covering school, home and social situations. Smaller versions can be laminated and attached to a key ring to enable the child to communicate in the playground or on the school bus. The pupil points to the appropriate picture, symbol or word in order to communicate with others. As far as possible the child should be in control of the communication board, should be able to use it in whatever way he/she wishes, and have little interference from adults or other children.

CASE STUDY — **Ali**

Ali is in Year 3. He has no functional speech but through facial expression and gesture he is a keen communicator. For the past six months he has been using a simple communication board, and he keeps it on his desk in class and also takes it home. It is made of a piece of laminated card with the symbols stuck on. Every six weeks or so his teacher adds one or two additional symbols as his communication develops, using Writing With Symbols software. Ali points to his board to answer questions, and to let the teacher or teaching assistant know what he wants or needs. To support his inclusion in lessons, each half term Ali's teacher and TA print off a small number of new symbols linked to class topics.

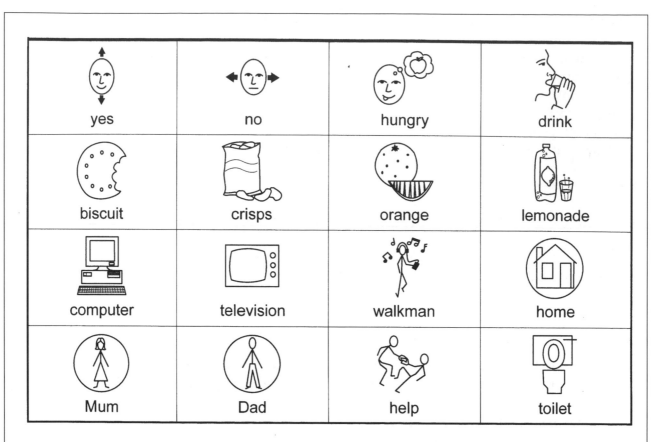

FIGURE 7.2 Ali's communication board

For young children, start with two photographs or pictures that relate to 'first' and 'then', such as, first you go to the toilet and then you go out to play, or first you finish your writing and then you can go on the computer. The use of the communication board can then be extended by adding additional tasks one at a time.

Communication book

A communication book contains separate symbols or words, each backed with Velcro. Ideal for this purpose is an inexpensive A5 peel-back photograph album. Each page holds the symbols for a particular category, such as foods, numbers, toys, and a strip of Velcro on the front of the communication book is used to display the symbols together and so create sentences or sequences of concepts. The pupil uses single symbols or a combination to communicate his/her ideas or to make requests.

Electronic communication aids

Some pupils with severe communication difficulties use a portable electronic communication device. These devices are usually based on a symbol system and can be very sophisticated. The child should always be in control of this communication aid. The child, not the teacher or teaching assistant, must be the one who decides when it is used. Effectively, the communication aid is the child's voice, and just as one would never cover a child's mouth to stop them speaking, so the communication aid should always be available for the child to use. It is important to give pupils time to create their sentence on the machine before you look away or repeat a question. There will need to be a member of staff in school who is trained to use the machine, and who is able to help the pupil with technical matters.

Symbols

All the time symbols are around us whether we are driving, at work or shopping in the supermarket; symbols are not just for people with learning difficulties. Many schools have found that developing the use of symbols across the curriculum has benefited many more pupils than solely those with special needs. Symbols support communication, independence, participation, literacy, creativity and access to information.

There are a number of symbol systems available for use in schools. The most effective way of developing the use of symbols is by installing Writing with Symbols 2000 (from Widgit Software) onto a computer. The program prints out symbols as the words are typed into a word processor. Grids of symbols are easy to create and can be used as communication boards. No additional training is needed for staff to help them understand the symbols as the word is printed below the symbol. This is a very simple way of making worksheets that are accessible for individual pupils. As with many resources designed for pupils with learning difficulties, the software has a much wider relevance. This is particularly the case for pupils with specific learning difficulties or other reading difficulties who benefit from having additional visual support with text.

Just as with any other new concept, symbols have to be taught before pupils can be expected to use them in any meaningful way.

Behaviour

Behaviour becomes a vital communication tool where pupils have limited ways to communicate their needs and wishes. It takes a long time to get to know a pupil well enough to decipher what they want from their behaviour alone, but it is wonderfully rewarding when understanding occurs. For pupils without an obvious or diagnosed disability it is always worth noting any change in behaviour patterns, as this could indicate an underlying problem.

CASE STUDY   **Ann**

Ann is in Year 6 of her local primary school. She has delayed speech and language, and learning difficulties. In recent weeks, Ann has been distracted in class and has begun to masturbate frequently and openly in school. Her teacher is very embarrassed by this behaviour and has contacted Ann's main carers who are her grandparents. They blame her new behaviour on the series of sex education lessons that has recently taken place. After six weeks of Ann being punished for this behaviour, her grandparents take her to see the GP who diagnoses a severe case of thrush, causing extreme itching. After a few days of treatment Ann is back to her usual self, and there are no more incidences of 'masturbation'.

If a pupil has behaviour problems, before putting it down to an 'in-child' reason always look at the possibility of an external cause. Most 'bad' behaviours are based on an environmental anxiety, such as a fear of a child or an adult in the class; or may be immature behaviours that were acceptable – and often reinforced – in the infants but which are not appropriate in the junior phase. Where the behaviour is related to a special educational need or disability, schools need to ensure that it does not cause discrimination against the child. On these situations the DRC Code of Practice gives guidance and advice, as well as useful exemplars.

Learning how to communicate with a child with learning difficulties successfully can be challenging, but is also hugely rewarding both personally and professionally. Mastering a few signs or incorporating symbols into your work may be only for one pupil initially, but those new skills will benefit many other children in the future.

Children with learning difficulties have a great deal of worth to say, they just need help to say it in a different way. Take the time to get to know these children, and share their ambitions and concerns. These are very special people and they might just surprise you!

The voice of the pupil with learning difficulties

Parents, teachers, doctors, psychologists, therapists: adults always *speak for* the child with learning difficulties. Right now we need to listen to what the child has to say. The United Nations Convention on the Rights of the Child (CSIE 1997) makes clear that we must begin to listen to the voice of the child much more directly, and the child's views must be given due weight when decisions are being made about his/her future.

Schools must move away from a paternalistic or sympathetic approach towards children with learning difficulties, and begin to look at the world through the eyes of those children. The time has come for schools and associated professions to take a more empathetic stance, with the pupil with learning difficulties at the centre of thinking and planning.

The appreciation that each child is an individual, each with distinctive gifts, talents, strengths, abilities and needs, will help schools become more responsive to the learning needs of all pupils.

Developing the pupil's voice

Children with learning difficulties need to learn how to be active participants in decision-making about their own lives. This process can begin as soon as a child starts school and should be developed as the child matures. By the time the children transfer to secondary school they should be used to participating in meetings about, and having a say in, decisions about their future.

Circle time

Circle time is a wonderful activity for developing the voice of the child. The emphasis on taking turns, affirmation and listening, supports the development of social and communication skills. Regular practice in speaking to a group and having what they say respected will help the child be confident enough to express their opinions and views in other situations, such as annual review meetings.

Reflection and self-assessment

Children need to learn how to reflect on their own work in school, and identify the areas they enjoy and those they find difficult. Clear and appropriate targets enable pupils to evaluate for themselves just what they have achieved. A completed reflection or self-assessment record for each half term can be added to the child's Experience Folder. This information should then be used for future planning and differentiation. Over time, supported self-assessment will build confidence, and the child will learn the skills required to offer opinions on class work and also on the social aspects of school. A pro forma that may be used to support self-assessment will be found on page 122.

Participation in annual review meetings

Annual reviews are daunting for parents and professionals and it is inappropriate to put children into such a potentially stressful situation. That does not mean, however, that the child's voice cannot be heard in the meeting. The child can be asked a series of questions before the meeting and the answers captured on video or audio tape. During the meeting this tape can be played to give those present information about how the child feels about school.

Questions such as:

- What do you like about school?
- What makes you feel proud?
- Who are your friends?
- What do you want to learn to do better?
- Are you worried about anything to do with school?
- Do you join any clubs or activities after school? Tell me about it.
- What do you look forward to doing in the future?

At the very least a photograph of the child should be displayed prominently, as this helps to focus attention on what is best for the child, and should help to prevent the meeting becoming bogged down in arguments.

The child's responses also can be recorded on paper using scribing or the draw and write method. A very straightforward 'What I want' form that includes a photograph will focus the adults' discussion again more directly on the pupil's priorities. A proforma of this form (Figure 7.4) is included on the accompanying CD.

The voice of the pupil without verbal communication

Some children with learning difficulties have no verbal communication, and so are unable to contribute their views in conventional ways. Sometimes it is assumed that they have no voice, but no matter their degree of learning difficulties, it is even more important for adults to 'listen', howsoever these children communicate. In order to hear that 'inner voice' it will be necessary for the adults involved to know the pupil well, as communication might be through signing, facial expression, gesture or behaviour.

It is not always straightforward to work out how much a pupil understands. Some pupils with learning difficulties have good expressive language but poor

Name _____ Date _____ Topic _____

In our topic . . .

I have learned that . . .

Now I can . . .

I liked . . .

I didn't like . . .

I want to get better at . . .

I would like this person to help me . . .

FIGURE 7.3   Self-assessment record

comprehension. Children with Williams Syndrome speak well with a good vocabulary, but their understanding of language is significantly delayed. The presumptions we make about a child's levels of understanding may not be accurate. Children may understand much less than we think, and need much more preparation and visual support, but their understanding may also be in advance of their expressive language, and so they will understand more than expected.

In order to hear the voice of pupils with profound and multiple learning difficulties teachers need to take time to observe how the pupil responds. Responses may include:

- change of direction of gaze;
- body movements towards or away from a stimulus;
- nodding or shaking the head;
- reaching out;
- grasping or pushing;
- smiles and laughter;
- crying.

Encourage children to make choices about day-to-day events: the kind of drink they would like, the music they want to listen to, with whom they want to spend time, etc. This day-to-day decision-making is vital if pupils are to develop greater independence.

Practical strategies

Below are practical suggestions for eliciting the voice of the child with learning difficulties. There can be no guarantee that these strategies will work for a particular child; try several approaches, or adapt them to fit the needs of your own pupils.

Questionnaires

Questionnaires are a very useful way of gauging how a pupil feels about issues in school. A combination of words, symbols, pictures and photographs will support understanding, and responses may be gauged using simply-drawn faces showing different emotions.

Smiley faces

Simple line drawings showing different facial expressions can be enormously useful to gauge a pupil's feelings about aspects of school. Happy and sad face cards or posters will give most pupils a way for them to tell you how they feel just by pointing, touching or turning towards one of the faces.

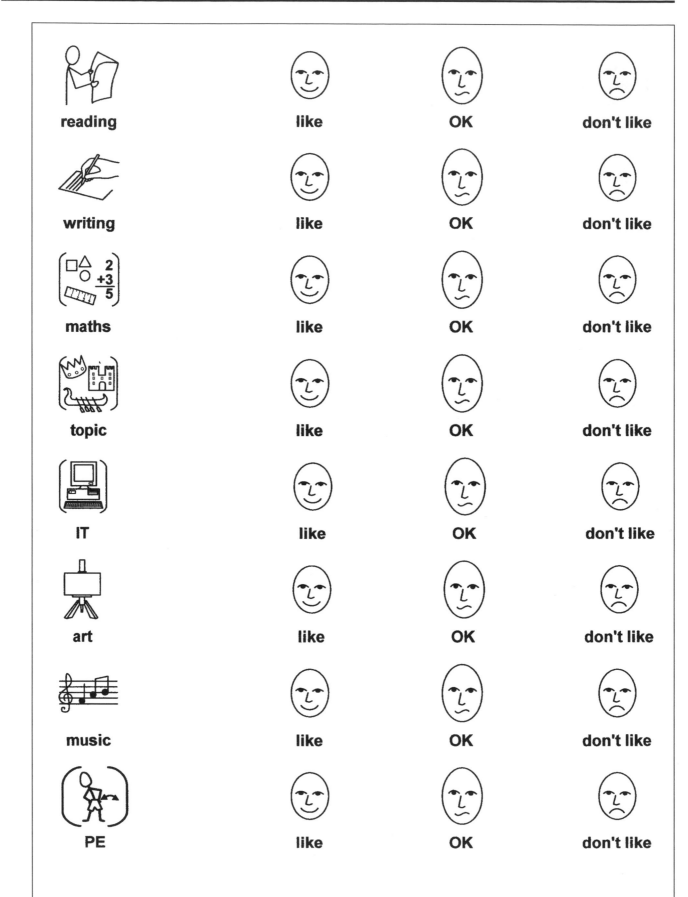

FIGURE 7.5 Symbol questionnaire

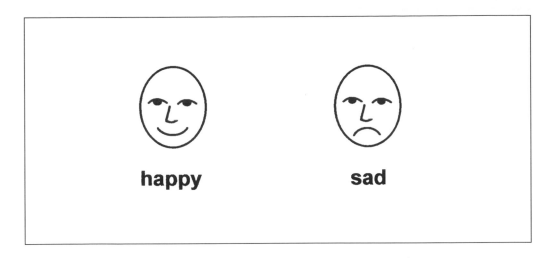

Computer programs such as Clicker 5 enable the faces to be displayed side-by-side on a computer screen. A mouse click, touch monitor or a point, may be used to select the face that matches how the pupil feels. The level of complexity is increased by adding additional faces with different expressions, but before they are used the meaning of these additional faces will need to be taught.

Signing

For some children with learning difficulties signing is the primary mode of expressive communication. Adults who support the pupil with learning difficulties to give his or her views must be able to sign – and understand signs – at the same level or better than the pupil. It may be necessary to involve a more expert signing communicator in order to draw out a pupil's precise meaning. This is especially important, as pupils with learning difficulties are rarely very precise signers themselves. Their signs have to be read in conjunction with context, vocalisations, facial expression and other gesture. A familiar and trusted adult who knows the pupil well is the ideal person to translate the child's wishes. Where no expert signer is available, a combination of signing and symbols, pictures or photographs is likely to be more successful than reliance on signing alone.

Symbols

Symbols have two distinct uses in supporting pupils to give their views. First, they can be used with, or instead of, text, to enable the pupil to understand information and questions. Second, they can be used by the pupil as a means of letting other people know what he/she wants. This might be through touching or pointing to symbols, sequencing them into sentences, or putting preferences into priority order. Communication cards with a simple format can be tailored to match the ability of individual pupils and situations, from two choices to a grid containing over a hundred symbols. Symbol choice or preference sheets are made very easily and pupils can colour in the different options using one colour to show they like the option or another colour to show they don't.

Traffic lights

All children are familiar with traffic lights and their meanings. A paper model of traffic lights is a fun way for pupils to say how they feel in simple terms about situations. A pupil responds to questions by pointing to or touching the requisite colour: green if they are happy for a situation to continue, amber if they are unsure or just not too keen, and red if definitely they want the situation to stop. Coloured discs are a variation of the traffic lights, and the pupil can lift up a disc and put it onto an object or picture.

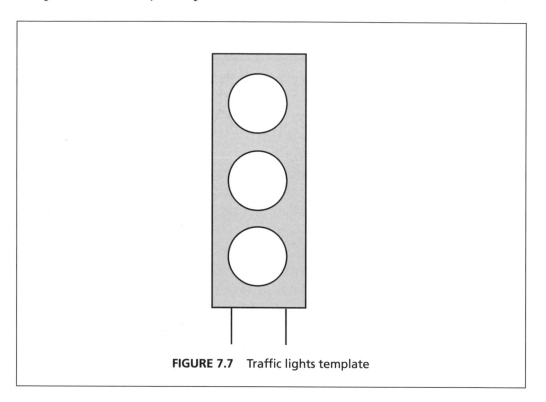

FIGURE 7.7   Traffic lights template

Comic strip conversations

These are conversations between two people facilitated by the use of simple drawings. The approach was introduced by Carol Gray (Gray 1994b) for pupils with autism and related disorders, but it works equally well for children with learning difficulties. The drawings are used to illustrate objects, people, places and feelings. Drawing at the same time as speaking has the added advantage of slowing adults down, and makes them easier to understand. Both the adult and the pupil draw as they speak. No artistic skills are required as stick figures are used for people and basic representations for everything else. Speech or thoughts are recorded in bubbles coming from the figures. Colours may be added to show different emotions (Gray 1994b). A focus on the drawing also minimises eye contact during the conversations, which some pupils with learning difficulties can find threatening. In the example below, Rageh has drawn himself in different situations in school.

FIGURE 7.8 Example of a comic strip conversation

Draw and write

In 'draw and write' the child is asked to draw a picture and then talk to an adult about what they have drawn. The adult writes the child's words onto the picture. Children might be asked to draw pictures about friends, school or a holiday. When a pupil is comfortable with the technique, the questions can be extended to develop self-reflection, such as, 'What do you do to make other people happy?' As with comic strip conversations, 'draw and write' takes the focus away from the adult's face and adds a visual component to spoken interactions. Because the pupil draws first, he/she has control of the discussion. This is preferable to the child merely responding to the adult's agenda. 'Draw and write' also creates a paper document that can be shared in meetings.

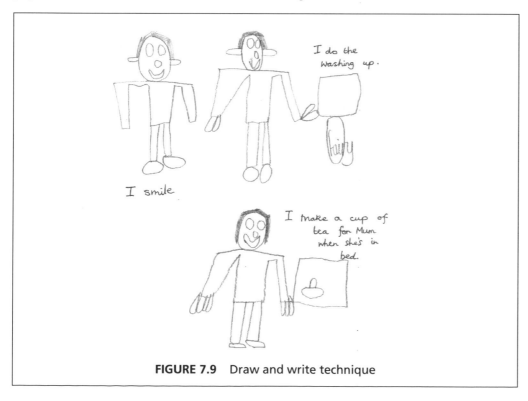

FIGURE 7.9 Draw and write technique

Cue cards

Cue cards may be used to encourage children to talk more fully about school-related events that have happened in the recent past. The cards can contain words, for example, first I . . . , then I . . . , in the end I . . . ; or symbols, such as a stick figure for people, a tree to represent the world outside, or faces to represent feelings. The cards help children to structure their thinking and narrative, with only minimal questioning by the adult. They act as prompts for ideas about people, talk, settings, feelings and consequences (Lewis 2002).

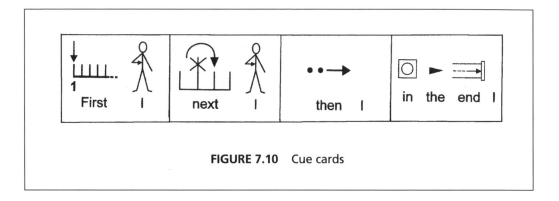

FIGURE 7.10   Cue cards

Mat techniques

Some children need a larger format for making choices. Mat techniques involve pupils moving to specific mats to show their preferences. They are also especially useful for pupils who have limited fine motor skills, but who can move by walking, crawling or shuffling. Plain mats are placed on the floor (PE mats or carpet samples are ideal), and numbers, words, photographs, symbols or pictures showing different facial expressions are stuck onto them. The pupil responds to a question by moving to the mat that represents his/her choice.

Speech and thought bubbles

Speech and thought bubbles are a fun way to record children's responses. 'Me' bubbles, with labels such as 'I can', 'I like', 'I am going to', 'I want', 'I don't like' give focus to questions. Focus initially on positive feelings and then move gradually to more negative statements.

Masks

The use of masks can help a pupil to talk about feelings, literally *from behind a mask*. The mask helps the child feel more confident to talk about school or personal matters. Masks can be bought from educational suppliers, but paper plates are much cheaper and just as effective. The children make their own masks, for they can then decide which emotion they want to show. Using the masks in role-play enables pupils to rehearse situations they find difficult. Children who do not like to wear masks, or who have limited speech, can be asked to choose a mask that shows how they feel about a particular situation.

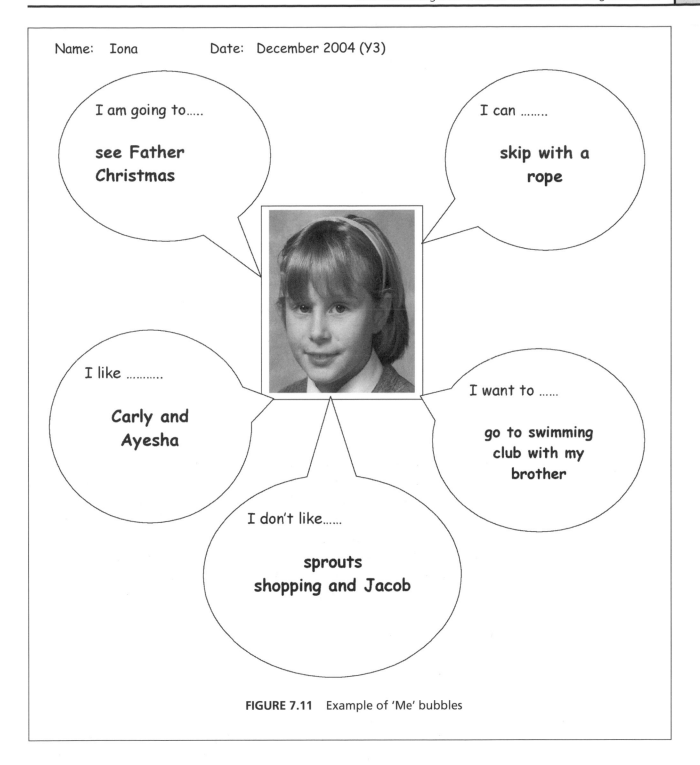

FIGURE 7.11 Example of 'Me' bubbles

Puppets

Puppets have long been used in the infant phase to support development of literacy skills and increasingly their use is being extended into junior classes. Puppets make lessons interactive, and children often find it easier to talk to or through a puppet. Small group sessions with the puppet are an ideal time for exploring how children feel and what they hope for in their future. Even though pupils know that it is the adult who is speaking and making the puppet move, many children still find it less threatening to interact with a puppet than with an adult. Use a video camera or audio tape to record the sessions so you can revisit them at a later time. A subsequent look at the tape often throws up new perspectives on how a child is feeling.

Gauging strength of feeling

Sometimes a teacher needs to gauge the depth of a pupil's feelings about a situation, and a visual and/or tactile strategy will give a more accurate measure than words alone. There are several ways this can be done, such as:

- squeezing toothpaste from a tube with the amount squeezed showing stronger or weaker feelings;
- unrolling a ball of string or ribbon;
- putting dried beans into a pot – the more beans there are, the stronger is the feeling;
- hanging smiley or sad faces, or ticking and crossing cards on a washing line to show how happy or how sad the pupil feels. (Lewis 2002)

A ladder laid down on the floor gives pupils a physical way of showing how strongly they feel about situations and/or how much they care. Put large numbers from one to ten between each of the rungs of the ladder. The pupil is then asked a question and is asked to move along a number of rungs, how much they do or do not want something to happen, or how much they do or do not like something.

Smart Alex (SEMERC)

Smart Alex is a computer program based on facial expression. The screen shows the head and shoulders of a child. The image can be configured to show a child who is a boy or a girl, with black or white skin. At the bottom of the screen is a grid showing words and/or symbols of different activities, animals and foods. The pupil clicks on a word or a symbol and Smart Alex's expression changes to show how the character feels about the choice. This program is excellent when used as a shared activity with another child or with an adult. The activity can be extended by prompting the child with questions such as, 'How does Alex feel now?' and 'What makes you feel like that?'

Concept Maps

Concept maps help children formulate their ideas by creating a visual plan. Words, pictures, photographs, symbols and different colours can be used accurately to reflect a child's feelings and wishes. Pupils with learning difficulties often have problems visualising abstract concepts, and concept maps make those ideas more accessible.

Self-books and films

An opportunity to be the star of their own story will have a big influence on children's self-esteem. Make a book about the child, as big and lavish as you like. Start by taking photographs of the pupil in different everyday situations. Then the child can dictate a narrative based on the photographs. Include other photographs of family and friends to give a more rounded portrayal of the child's life. Create additional books to support the child through times of change, such as the transfer to a new class or to secondary school.

Support children to make up stories about imaginary children who experience similar problems to their own. This helps them understand that other people have the same difficulties, and the fictional basis adds objectivity to familiar situations and events. Reading about events in the third person helps some children to talk through the problems they experience without talking directly about themselves.

All children want to star in a film – and making a film in school gives them the chance. With digital video cameras now available in most schools a film of the pupil can be made in a similar way to the self-books. If videos of pupils are to be taken, parents must be informed and permission sought.

Posters

Some children have big characters and need to work on a bigger scale. Create a poster with the pupils showing aspects of their life with key words, or symbols and 'feelings' written in different colours to show how they feel about each aspect. Include photographs or the child's own drawings, and make visual links between ideas and feelings by using arrows or coloured lines. Add thought and speech bubbles to show the pupil's own words.

Poems

Poetry uniquely creates emotional and conceptual opportunities, because it frees children with learning difficulties from the constraints of sentence construction by utilising individual words and short phrases. Give the pupil an object or a picture to hold. The pupil then dictates words and phrases relating to the object or picture, starting with descriptive words, and then moving to more emotional language. Acrostics are a good starting point as the initial sounds give phonic prompts, such as in the poem below by Frankie writing about his dog, Buster.

> *'Buster' by Frankie*
> B – big and black
> U – under my covers
> S – shiny
> T – tongue
> E – excited
> R – running fast

Frankie began to cry as soon as his poem finished and he told his teacher that Buster had been ill and had to be taken to the vet every week for injections. Frankie's usual demeanour gave no indication of his worry about his dog, but the poem brought his feelings to the surface, and his teacher and friends were able to support him through a difficult time.

Facial expression photographs and drawings

Facial expression photographs are available from several educational resource suppliers, but they are very expensive. A more cost-effective alternative is to make your own set using a digital camera. Photograph children making different facial expressions, starting with happy and sad. Gradually build up the range of expressions to include worried, angry, disappointed, surprised – the list is endless. This makes an excellent project in PSHE and is great fun for all the class. Laminate the photographs to protect them from damage so they can be used over and over again.

Drama, role-play and dance

Drama and role-play offer children the opportunity to work through and rehearse situations and emotions with people they trust. Drama broadens the range of emotional expression, incorporates facial expression, movement and words, and allows children to practise different forms of interaction. In the same way, dance introduces pupils to an additional medium of communication by developing new body shapes, gestures and movements. Through drama and dance pupils with limited verbal communication are able to transmit their feelings both effectively and creatively.

Role-play is a very powerful medium that will help pupils with learning difficulties practise different and more appropriate responses to the situations they find difficult. Some caution needs to be exercised, as a pupil may become distressed at 'reliving' situations they find painful or uncomfortable.

Summary

Hearing and listening to the voice of the child with learning difficulties will take time and effort. But taking the trouble to hear what they have to say, by whatever means, will always be worthwhile. Most people with learning difficulties know what they want from life, and their aspirations are much like those of everyone else: to be loved, to be safe, to have a home and a family, to be respected. If one strategy does not work, try another, and another, and keep on trying. Children with learning difficulties have a lot to say – we just have to learn how to listen and hear what they say.

Chapter 8 looks at the inclusion challenges and opportunities of transitions.

Transitions: inclusion challenges and opportunities

Times of change and transition are potentially stressful periods for all children. Stress is often significant, particularly for children with learning difficulties. Not all children will have difficulties with transitions, and so may not need additional support. The trouble is that we don't know beforehand *which* children will find it hard, or *which* situation will spark off the anxiety – so we should anticipate and plan for transitions however a child may have reacted in the past.

Any transition has the potential to trigger anxiety resulting in a serious deterioration of self-esteem and behaviour. While we expect the transfer from primary to secondary school to cause anxiety, other, more frequent changes and transitions also have a potential to upset the child's equilibrium. This does not mean that children need to be sheltered from transitions and change; they need to be prepared for and supported through the transition. This is not a one-way street, with all the onus on the child to adapt; schools must examine their own situations and systems in order the better to meet individual needs.

Planning transitions

Successful transitions do not just happen – it is no good 'waiting to see how he fits in' because the probability is that he won't! When the child does kick off because he is anxious, it is he who will get the blame for inappropriate or challenging behaviour. If the school has not made reasonable adjustments for the transition or change, however, it is not the child's fault if the situation breaks down.

The time commitment necessary to plan transitions may seem a burden to teachers, but an hour spent with colleagues on working out a strategy to support a child through a period of change will save disruption to other children, and avoids many hours of future work writing behaviour plans, meeting with educational psychologists, talking to parents, and so on.

Whether the plan is for a big change, such as the move from the nursery into reception class, or simply a change from one activity to another, it must be planned in some detail, and the child pre-warned and prepared. Create a written plan shared with the child's parents and the other members of the classroom team. This ensures that everyone working with the child is 'singing from the same hymn sheet' and boosts everyone's confidence that the child can be supported through the transition. This confidence is especially important when a child has had past difficulties with change and transition, which will make staff, understandably, feel apprehensive.

Pupil involvement

Even very young children can be involved in the transition planning process and the more involved the child, the greater the chance of success. The child will feel more confident when working through the transition *with* others, rather than being forced into a new situation *by* others. Tell the child about impending changes and make it into an exciting adventure. Create picture books about the new situation using photographs of the child acting out what he/she will do and how he/she will feel in the new setting or after the change.

CASE STUDY — **Yassim**

Yassim transferred from his primary school to the secondary school on the same site. During Year 6 his behaviour deteriorated significantly as he become more and more anxious about the move to the new school – even though it was just next door. Yassim's parents, his class teacher and the SENCO from the secondary school met to decide how to support him through the transition and hoped to lessen his anxiety. A week after the meeting Yassim and a teaching assistant visited the secondary school. They were given a tour of the campus and Yassim was photographed in different rooms in the school: the science laboratory, the sports hall, the canteen, the library. These photographs were then put into a book and Yassim wrote sentences underneath about what he had seen. He took the book home to share with his family and added other pictures and information about the school. During the visit Yassim was also told that Year 9 pupils would have the opportunity to go on a French exchange trip. This French exchange became a focus for Yassim throughout the transition, and he began to understand the positive aspects of the new school and to look forward to going there.

Pre-school to mainstream primary school

Most young children take in their stride the transfer to reception class, especially as the foundation stage curriculum is continued into reception, and also the new activities are based on play and exploration. For some children, however, the change in routine and personnel will be a challenge and some additional visits and accommodations will be necessary.

Preparatory visits

Nursery or playgroup visits
Commonly it is good practice for reception class teachers to invite nursery classes to visit the school. This gives an opportunity to spend time in reception with familiar children and adults, builds confidence and creates positive associations, all without singling out the pupil with special needs.

Parental visits
Most parents of children with learning difficulties choose to send their child to the primary school nearest to home. This allows the child to be part of the local

community, and fosters opportunities for contacts with other children outside school. Parents are likely to feel very anxious at this first visit, and will be just as interested in a friendly atmosphere and calm environment as in the school's place in the league table. But parents of children with learning difficulties will be interested in league table results too, like all other parents, because they also want their child to go to a good school.

This first visit by parents is crucial to the future success of the placement, and it is best if parents visit without their child on this occasion. They can then better observe the school environment without worrying about the child's reaction to new surroundings, and they may discuss their hopes and concerns more freely with the teacher. Invite parents to sit in a lesson for a while so that later they can tell their child all about it. Build in time to talk to new parents, find out about the child and give information about the class and the school's expectations.

Give parents photographs of the teacher, teaching assistant and children in the reception class to take home to share with the child. These can be stuck into a scrapbook about the new school and will be the start of the preparation for transition. Ask parents to bring with them an object that is familiar to the child to leave in the classroom – such as a picture, a soft toy or a favourite book – and this will provide a link between school and home when the child visits.

Pupil visits

The first visit

The first visit by the child and parents together is best timetabled to take place after the other pupils have left at the end of the school day. Coming to terms with the size and layout of the buildings before having to deal with the social demands of the school is very helpful. Encourage parents to take photos of their child in the new class, in the hall, in the playground and other areas of the school. The child can then look at the photographs and ask questions at home. These pictures should be added to the scrapbook about the school.

The second joint visit

This should follow on quite soon after the first joint visit, and should take place during the school day. The visit should be unhurried, with plenty of opportunities for everyone to ask questions. The child should not be expected to take part in any activities at this stage. A prospective pupil will best be left to watch and absorb the atmosphere in the security of their parents' company. Any access issues should be discussed at this visit, giving the school plenty of time to make the necessary reasonable adjustments

.

Joining Year R lessons

Regular weekly visits need to take place during the term before entry. These visits should include time spent in class, outside in the playground, in the library, in the hall; the child could even be invited to stay for lunch on a couple of occasions.

Towards the end of the term give the child a place to keep personal belongings – a drawer or a box in a cupboard – and fill it with some favourite activities, paper and pens, a puzzle or a book. These familiar items will help the child to settle more quickly into the reception class.

A video of the school

A short video of a school day will give the pupil something to watch at home and prepare for the transition. This video will help the family begin to talk about the new school, and will build awareness and realistic expectations of how the school operates.

Time spent preparing for entry is never wasted, because the more comfortable and confident a child feels about their new school, the more successful will be the long-term placement.

CASE STUDY | **Jason**

Jason is four years and ten months old and he has global developmental delay. As yet Jason has no specific diagnosis other than that he is delayed by approximately two years in most areas of development, and has a more significant delay in speech and language.

From the age of three Jason attended a mainstream nursery with adult support for three sessions each week. That placement has been successful and Jason's parents have developed a close and trusting working relationship with the staff. Jason has made progress at the nursery and now knows most colours and can count to five. He communicates using some vocalisation and a small number of Signalong signs. He is fully mobile and can walk up and down stairs without support, but he is still in pads.

He is beginning to initiate some interactions with the children at nursery and he plays happily with his younger brother at home. Jason's parents want him now to transfer to the mainstream school just around the corner from the family home.

Liaison between reception class teacher and nursery staff started in the term before entry, especially with the adult who has supported Jason for the past two years. Alongside their detailed records of Jason's progress against the Foundation Stage Stepping Stones and against the P scales, the nursery has kept a photographic record of his experiences and responses. This information, together with the teacher's own observations of Jason, enabled the school to plan adjustments to:

- the curriculum (planning and schemes of work to include Jason's learning needs);
- assessment (obtaining a copy of the P scales document);
- resources (Writing with Symbols software);
- training (Signalong signing);
- liaison with the speech and language therapy service;
- the building (a toilet for disabled people) to ensure access for Jason.

Uniform

An exciting part of the move to school is having new clothes or a uniform to wear. If the school has a uniform, allow the child with learning difficulties to wear it when visiting the school. This will help him/her to feel more grown up and a part of the school community.

The first day in the new school

The child with learning difficulties most likely will have visited the school on several occasions, so ask him/her to help by being a partner for another child on the first day. This serves two purposes. First, the pupil will be pleased to be given responsibility and will gain self-esteem; second, other pupils will have a positive first impression of their classmate who has learning difficulties.

Where the pupil has a teaching assistant, try not to make the support too overt, especially on that first day. The pupil needs to become used to being independent in the classroom and it is best to start as you mean to go on. This is also important in determining how the pupil is perceived by others. All the children will be unsure in the new classroom, and if they are encouraged to help each other, they will naturally play with and include the pupil with learning difficulties.

Social stories

Social stories (Gray 1994a) are a valuable tool for helping children with learning difficulties to settle into a new setting. The teacher and parents write the story, giving as much information as the child needs. A social story about a new school could be:

> I go to school to learn and to play with the other children. All children go to school. Sometimes I can choose what I do and sometimes I must do what my teacher tells me to do. Daddy will take me to school and then go to work. Mummy will pick me up in the car when school is finished.

A social story describes a situation or concept, and gives relevant social cues and a perspective that informs and supports children with learning difficulties. The story can be introduced at home or at school, and should be read regularly at a frequency appropriate for the individual child. Stories can be extended or renewed as the child's confidence and skills develop.

Moving to a new class

A reality of working with children with learning difficulties is that their behaviour can be very different from one situation to another. A child may exhibit challenging behaviour in one class, and yet be as good as gold in another. But the child hasn't changed and the class hasn't changed; the basis of the difference lies in the change of location and personnel.

Location

A primary classroom is a very important place, the place where, after their home, children spend most time. At different times that classroom is a workplace, a refuge, a prison, a party venue, a playroom, and a home from home. After a whole year in that room everything will be familiar and 'comfortable', and children will be both reluctant and excited to move on to a new class. Start to prepare for a change of location at the beginning of the summer term, right after

Easter. Introduce the transition into class discussions and encourage the children to talk about their feelings regarding the impending change. Plan ways for the child with learning difficulties to 'visit' the new classroom for short periods of time – such as taking a message, returning a book, or sharing a piece of equipment. Organise joint class activities such as an art day or a geography day and base this day on a particular country or terrain (the rain forest or the arctic) where the children from the two classes can work on activities in both rooms. Make sure favourite books are in the book corner, and let the child choose the picture or symbol for his/her coat-peg. These positive associations will develop the children's confidence and there will be excitement about the move to the new classroom.

Personnel

Primary teachers are hugely influential in the lives of their pupils, probably far more influential than is realised. Helping a class to work not only as a set of 30 or more individuals but also as a cohesive group is very important in that first term, just as is the content of the lessons. As with all relationships, it takes time to build a shared understanding and trust with all those new little people. Try to get to know the child with learning difficulties in the term before they move to your class, as the better the relationship between teacher and child the easier will be the transition. This need not take up additional time or effort – just make a point of saying hello, chat with the child when you are on playground duty, and smile at him/her!

A home visit is probably the most valuably effective single action a new teacher can make. To know a child in the school context is one thing, but finding out about the child at home will give a much broader perspective. A visit will make the child feel special and help him/her understand that you care about him/her and the family. Parents will also be very grateful for an opportunity to talk to a teacher on their own patch, away from the necessary formalities of school.

Where the class or the child is to be supported by a teaching assistant, that TA should be included in both getting to know the child and also in the home visit. This 'united front' will give confidence to the child and to the parents, and the more confident the family, the more successful the transition to the new class.

The move to a new class is a major change in a child's life. An additional change of teaching assistant can lead to anxiety and inappropriate behaviour. Try to maintain the pupil's contact with at least one well-known teaching assistant during these transitions, and wait until the child is settled in the new class before changing support personnel.

Small schools

In small primary schools, where several year groups are taught together in each class, a move up a class will mean moving to a group that includes some older children. This means that the gap in ability between the child with learning difficulties and the oldest children is very wide indeed.

In this situation a decision is often made to delay the move, or to stagger it over a period of time. In such cases the child with learning difficulties joins the new class for non-academic lessons such as art or music, and stays with the younger class for literacy and numeracy. In theory this does appear to be a practical solution but in practice it is not a good idea, for several reasons:

1. the child with learning difficulties is left unsure as to which class they really belong;
2. the other children in the class do not get to know their new classmate;
3. the child's difference is reinforced;
4. the child misses out on the breadth of the curriculum and effectively repeats work already covered;
5. it will be harder for the child when they have to transfer to the new class full-time.

Where a child with learning difficulties is an established member of a class in reception he/she should move up right through the school with that same group of children. That is the child's class and that is where he/she belongs.

Moving from one activity to another

Some pupils with learning difficulties find it difficult to stop one activity and move on to another, especially if they are involved in a favourite activity or not too keen on the activity that is to happen next. These situations can lead to oppositional behaviour and disruption for the whole class. The more a child is forced to do something against their will, the more set become the oppositional behaviours.

To solve these difficulties plan for the pupil to have short periods of involvement with required activities interspersed with activities they particularly enjoy (Seach *et al.* 2002). Teach the concept of time passing using a symbolic schedule or, for more able pupils, a diary. The schedule shows the pupil the sequence of activities throughout the lesson or the day, so they can see what will happen when they finish the current activity and can see something just as nice coming up soon.

CASE STUDY **Jenny**

Jenny always becomes upset on Friday morning when it is time to go into assembly. Her TA made a visual schedule for her using symbols mounted on cardboard and backed with Velcro. Her schedule for Friday morning shows:

> reading   writing   assembly   snack time   play

Once Jenny could actually *see* that after assembly it would be time for her snack and then play, she was much more willing to go into the hall with her class. She carried her schedule into assembly and her TA pointed to the snack and play symbols whenever she became anxious or agitated. Jenny also took the carpet square that she uses when sitting on the floor in the classroom into the hall for assembly. This made her more comfortable than on the hard wooden floor in the hall and gave her a physical boundary, 'her place', in which to sit.

Assemblies

Assemblies, dinner times, and other large school gatherings cause some children to become very upset, perhaps because of the noise, the larger space in the hall, or just because of the large number of people together. It is not possible to control this particular environment for the child with learning difficulties, but it is possible to give the child a device that helps him/her cope with the situation. If a child finds the hall too noisy offer him/her a portable tape or CD player with a favourite piece of music or a story to listen to. For some children wearing their coat with the hood up will help to muffle the noise, and block out part of the visual stimulus.

Symbol timetables and schedules

Symbol timetables introduce children to the concept of 'what comes next'. For young children a very simple schedule of just two symbols may be appropriate, showing what is happening now and what is to happen next.

A symbol timetable has the added advantage of being very flexible, and should there be an unexpected change to the routine, the cards can be hastily rearranged to reflect the new situation. Creating a timetable at the start of the day or lesson is an enjoyable activity for a child which can be shared with the teacher or teaching assistant. Pupils are far more motivated independently to work through the activities if they are involved in planning their own schedules. This interactive time can also be used to review the daily routine, discuss changes, and reinforce rules (Smith-Myles and Simpson 1998).

Encourage pupils to interact with their schedule by crossing off activities once they are finished, or by removing cards and putting them into a 'finished' box. A surprise 'mystery' '?' symbol can be used as an exciting way to accustom children to unexpected events. Be sure to intersperse the required work with favourite activities and free time, and build in rewards throughout the session.

A short and regular transition ritual will serve to break up the lesson into smaller more manageable segments, and refocus the child on the new activity. A transition ritual happens after one activity is completed and before the next one begins, and may take the form of a breathing exercise, physical movement (a Brain Gym activity is ideal), a particular piece of music or song, or a special object (Clements and Zarkowska 2000).

Schools are not regimented places and often things do not go to plan. With visual support most children with learning difficulties cope well with the class-room routine, but may have particular difficulties when something they were looking forward to doesn't happen – sports day is rained off or the swimming pool is closed. You can teach the child a 'disappointment routine' – what to do when things do not go as expected (Clements and Zarkowska 2000). This might be to fetch a box in the cupboard with 'special' games and activities, or to go to the head teacher's office for ten minutes: any activity that the child enjoys and that will distract him/her from disappointment.

Graded change

Graded change techniques over time will help children to develop a tolerance of change by gradually altering the minor aspects of a situation, event or activity, one step at a time. It is vital that the changes are made predictable for the pupil by using visual cues (Howlin and Rutter 1987), such as a symbol schedule. The changes can then be increased as the child builds up some tolerance of uncertainty. When you tell children about a future event or activity that you cannot guarantee absolutely – 'We will have sports day on Wednesday' or 'The chicks will hatch next week' – this should be made clear by adding 'probably', 'maybe' or 'I hope that'. Teach the children what these words and phrases mean (Sainsbury 2000).

The concept of time

Children with learning difficulties very often have an impaired understanding of time – that awareness which most children develop of how long a lesson or a school day will last. Children need to be reassured by letting them know what is going to happen next, and when the next pleasurable activity is going to happen. Kitchen or sand timers are useful resources because they allow children to see how much longer they have left upon a particular activity and, when the timer rings or the sand runs out, they know it is time to move on to something else. When children are able to match, clock faces may also be used on their schedule, which can be checked with the clock on the wall. Try using two clocks: one with the 'now' time and, with the hands on the second clock set to the time at the end of the session or activity – 'then' (Parker 2000).

For weekly sessions, such as speech and language therapy or physiotherapy, a colourful timeline is useful. This will help children to understand when and how many times a series of activities will be repeated over a period of time. Mark the timeline out to show the days of the week and highlight the relevant days in a different colour. Add a picture of something the child particularly likes, such as a van, a frog or a train, and then move it from one highlighted day to the next at the end of every session. This gives the child a visual representation of time passing and helps him/her to anticipate future events (Aarons and Gittens 1998).

The use of a schedule to structure a day, or merely a lesson, significantly reduces a child's anxiety and improves behaviour. The rule of thumb is the more anxious the child, the greater the degree of visual structure necessary. As the child grows in confidence in the classroom so the level of visual structure can be diminished. Equally, should a child's level of anxiety increase for any reason, the level of visual structure will need to be increased.

'Finished'

Sometimes, children do not understand the concept of 'finished'. Teaching this and reinforcing it with an object of reference, sign or symbol will help the pupil understand when one activity ends and another begins.

> **CASE STUDY** **Karin**
>
> Karin is in Year 1. She has Autistic Spectrum Disorder and learning difficulties. Karin can read a small number of words, write her name, and she loves colouring in. Karin frequently becomes 'stuck' on an activity, particularly colouring, and refuses to stop, becoming more and more upset and usually ending in a full-blown tantrum.
>
> Her teacher prepares a series of see-through plastic wallets, each containing an activity. Some of the activities are for Karin to work through independently and some are paired or TA-supported work. Karin is shown the wallets and each activity explained, with every alternate wallet containing a small A5 picture for her to colour and some felt tip pens. The final wallet contains Karin's snack biscuit.

Organise the child's work space to show a clearly marked place for finished work. A box or a folder will do, but for children who need a more definite 'finished' a small swing bin at the side of the desk is ideal. Finished work is put into the bin and the child can no longer see it or touch it – the only disadvantage is that you have to teach the rest of the class not to put their empty crisp packets in there!

The transition from special school to mainstream

There is an increasing number of children now who start their education in a special school, and later transfer to a mainstream primary school. For a child with learning difficulties, more used to a small class with a high level of adult support, this transition will be a huge step. In this situation a gradual integration into the mainstream class is usually more appropriate.

A planned gradual transfer into a mainstream class is the most effective way of developing successful inclusion. The transfer is a big thing for the child, for the teacher, and especially for the other children in the class. The impact on the other children can be overlooked in the concern to get the curriculum and access issues right. Suddenly to have a new child in class who may look different, act different, and who is treated differently – not to mention a new teaching assistant – is a lot to expect young children to assimilate.

Make as positive as possible those first contacts between the child with learning difficulties and the rest of the class. Plan the first visits to coincide with a sports day, a dance festival, or a Christmas party. Praise the other children for their friendly behaviour and for being helpful. Explain that this child is to join their class and that you want their assistance in planning a special welcome. Take them to visit the child in the special school, and have them join in games and use some of the facilities, such as a ball pool.

Very close liaison with the parents, the special school class teacher and the support agencies and therapists is an important part of the transition process. This co-operation often has very positive spin-offs, with joint projects and topics being shared between the two schools and a wealth of expertise within the special school staff on which to call. A speech and language therapist may formulate a communication programme for one child, and those skills developed by teachers and teaching assistants through working with the therapist will be used for other children in the future.

Transitions from primary to secondary school

Year 5 annual review of statement

The Year 5 annual review is the crucial meeting for planning the transition from primary to secondary school. Poor communication and insufficient planning at this stage are the most common reasons for later unsuccessful placements. This meeting must be attended by:

- the parents;
- the teacher;
- teaching assistants who work with the child;
- the head teacher;
- the primary school SENCO;
- the SENCOs from any possible secondary schools;
- key professionals from other agencies, depending on a child's needs – educational psychologist, speech and language therapist, physiotherapist, occupation therapist, learning support service teacher – whoever is involved with the child;
- the child must be represented in some way, on paper, video, tape recorder, or in person for at least part of the meeting.

The meeting must decide on a positive course of action that gives the secondary school a plan from which to make any necessary amendments in terms of physical or curriculum access, and which will enable the primary school and parents to prepare the child for the transition.

The most important decision for the meeting to make is 'who will co-ordinate the transition'. This must be one person based in the primary school who takes on the responsibility for liaising between the schools and the parents. Without this close liaison and co-ordination some children will fall between the gaps.

> **CASE STUDY** | **Shanta**
>
> Shanta's primary school invited the SENCOs from the two local secondary schools to her Year 5 annual review. Shanta's mum told the meeting which school she preferred, and the high school SENCO and the LEA officer present agreed that Shanta's needs could be met in that school. Because of this positive meeting Shanta's mum assumed that the statement would be amended to name the school of her choice, and so she did not fill in the parental preference forms. However the LEA named a different school for Shanta because of a breakdown in communication between the LEA SEN team and the admissions team. Shanta eventually went to the school of her choice, but only after a great deal of worry and turmoil for her family.

Mainstream placements for children with learning difficulties often stop at the transition from primary to secondary school. This might be because the child's parents feel the secondary school is not an appropriate place for their child or that the teachers in the primary school may believe that a move to a special school would be better for the child. There are many concerns voiced, such as:

- **The child 'wouldn't cope' in a mainstream secondary school**

  It isn't up to the child with learning difficulties to 'cope' in the secondary school. It is the responsibility of the school to change to meet the needs of a more diverse population of children, and to give the child the necessary support to be able to succeed.

- **The secondary school curriculum is not appropriate for a child with learning difficulties**

  The schools' own access plan must identify how the curriculum is to be made accessible for all children. By using the tracking back, key concepts or curriculum overlapping techniques – and a little creativity and teamwork – the curriculum can be adapted to meet the needs of children with learning difficulties.

- **The child does not have the personal organisation to be able to move from class to class after each lesson**

  There are many children who struggle for the first few weeks to find their way around a large school, but eventually they become familiar with the layout of the site and settle to the new system. It may take a bit longer for children with learning difficulties, but with a little support from adults and other pupils, they too will learn the routine. Some secondary schools organise Year 7 more in a primary model, where the children stay in their classroom base for maths, English, French, history, geography, RE and PSHE, but have science lessons in the laboratories, IT in the computer suite, and PE in the gym. Over the course of Year 7 more and more lessons are taken away from the base, until by the start of Year 8 the children have the confidence and skills to move from class to class.

- **The child would be bullied**

  This is a major concern for parents and primary school teachers alike. But what kind of communities are our secondary schools if we are afraid to send children there? Schools must have robust anti-bullying policies and should support any vulnerable pupils to keep them safe. Often the perception and fear of bullying is much greater than the reality, and most children with special educational needs are happy and safe in their schools. For schools really to be safe and pleasant places, we ought to work towards inclusion so that we create safe and pleasant schools for every child.

- **Secondary school teachers only teach their subjects, they aren't SEN teachers**

  All teachers are teachers of children with special educational needs no matter in which phase they work or which subject they teach. All teachers who have trained in the past five years will expect a diverse range of pupils in their classes.

- **The secondary school doesn't have a hydrotherapy pool**

  Hydrotherapy pools are a great resource, both fun and therapeutic, but this therapy is essential only for a small number of children with additional physical needs. The educational choices made on behalf of a child should not hang on the availability of a hydro pool! When hydrotherapy is recommended for a child, link up with a local special school. The child should be able to access this pool during a games afternoon or outside school hours.

- **The children in the special school go horse riding**

  Some Riding for the Disabled (RDA) groups are now open after school hours or during the weekends, so that children with learning difficulties who attend mainstream schools can use the facilities with their parents. RDA is a wonderful activity and many children develop new skills in the sessions, but again, it is not sufficiently important to base a child's education on such a facility.

- **The child would not have a peer group**
  Children who have been included successfully in a mainstream primary school already have a peer group with which to move up to the secondary school. Good schools that foster respect for diversity and celebrate all achievement will encourage that peer group to be maintained into adolescence. It is positive for children with learning difficulties to meet other people who are disabled, or who have a similar learning difficulty, but this will happen through parent support groups or clubs in the evening.
- **Children at the special school can stay there until they are nineteen**
  An important part of growing and maturing is having the opportunity to experience new situations and new people. At age sixteen many young people with learning difficulties are ready for a different style of educational experience. The transfer to further education should be seen as a positive step, especially as local further education colleges offer a range of entry and pre-entry level courses for young people of all abilities. These courses include and allow a continued focus on basic literacy, numeracy, and life skills. In addition the young people learn new skills which prepare them for the world of work.

The reality is that parents have the right to choose a mainstream secondary school placement for their child. A positive lead from the primary school will help the teachers in the high school to accept the child, and the transition in the long term will prove more successful with a joint approach between both schools.

Supporting children through the transition from primary to secondary school

The move to a new school is a major change in a child's life. An additional change of teaching assistant may lead to anxiety and inappropriate behaviour. If possible, arrange for a teaching assistant from the primary school to move across to the secondary school with the child for the first few weeks of Year 7. This gives the pupil support through the transition from an adult they know and trust, and the teaching assistant is able to work alongside the secondary school staff and pass on knowledge and understanding. The short-term cost implications of this system need to be balanced by the savings likely to be made from a pupil experiencing fewer difficulties in the longer term.

Peer support

Other children are the most effective form of support for a child with learning difficulties through transfer from primary to secondary school. A buddy scheme or Circle of Friends that is set up during Year 6 and carried over into Year 7 will provide the necessary continuity and will help the child to settle more quickly. Where only one or two members of the buddy scheme transfer to the same school as the child with learning difficulties, those children can form a nucleus of the new buddies or Circle of Friends.

Summary

All children have to move through major changes and transitions throughout the primary years and into secondary school. We cannot avoid these changes and transitions for children with learning difficulties, but we can ease the way for the child, and we can prepare the child the better to manage in new situations. Whatever steps schools take to help children with learning difficulties through transitions will also help other children who may be less confident, or who have other difficulties in their lives. The reasonable adjustments made for one child will 'clear the ramp' for all the others.

References and suggested further reading

Aarons, M. and Gittens, T. (1998) *Autism: A Social Skills Approach for Children and Adolescents*. London: Wilmslow.

Alton, S., Beadman, J., Black, B., Lorenz, S. and McKinnon, C. (2003) *Education Support Pack for Schools*. London: Down's Syndrome Association.

Aronson, E. and Patnoe, S. (1997) *The Jigsaw Classroom: Building Cooperation in the Classroom*. New York: Addison Wesley Longman.

Booth, T., Ainscow, M., Black-Hawkins, K., Vaughan, M. and Shaw, L. (2000) *Index for Inclusion: Developing Learning and Participation in Schools*. Bristol: Centre for Studies in Inclusive Education (CSIE).

Brown, E. (1994) *Handa's Surprise*. London: Walker Books.

Buzan, T. (2003) *Mind Maps for Kids*. London: Thorsons.

Carpenter, B., Ashdown, R. and Bovair, K. (1996) *Enabling Access: Effective Teaching and Learning for Pupils with Learning Ddifficulties*. London: David Fulton.

Centre for Studies on Inclusive Education (CSIE) (1997) *Inclusive Education: A Framework for Change*. Bristol: CSIE.

Cheminais, R. (2002) *Inclusion and School Improvement: A Practical Guide*. London: David Fulton.

Clements, J. and Zarkowska, E. (2000*) Behavioural Concerns and Autistic Spectrum Disorders*. London: Jessica Kingsley.

Cohen, I. and Goldsmith, M. (2000) *Hands On: How to Use Brain Gym® in the Classroom*. Ventura, CA: Edu-Kinesthetics, Inc.

Department for Education and Employment (1999) *The National Curriculum: Handbook for Primary Teachers in England*. London: DfEE.

Department for Education and Skills (2001) *Special Educational Needs Code of Practice*. London: DfES.

Department for Education and Skills (2002) *National Numeracy Strategy: Towards the National Curriculum for Mathematics*. London: DfES.

Disability Rights Commission (2002) *Code of Practice for Schools: Disability Discrimination Act 1995: Part 4*. London: The Stationery Office.

East, V. and Evans, L. (2003) *At a Glance: A Quick Guide to Children's Special Needs*. Birmingham: Questions Publishing.

Edwards, S. (2001) *Independence for All: Strategies for Including Pupils with Special Educational Needs*. Tamworth: NASEN.

Fagg, S., Aherne, P., Skelton, S. and Thornber, A. (1990) *Entitlement for All in Practice*. London: David Fulton.

Faupel, A., Herrick, E. and Sharp, P. (1998) *Anger Management: A Practical Guide*. London: David Fulton.

Fox, G. (1993) *A Handbook for Special Needs Assistants: Working in Partnership with Teachers*. London: David Fulton.

Frost, L., and Bondy, A. (1998) 'The picture exchange communication system'. Seminars in *Speech and Language Therapy*, **19**, 373–89.

Giangreco, M. F., Cloninger, C. J, and Iverson, V. S. (1998) *Choosing Outcomes and Accommodations for Children (COACH): A Guide to Educational Planning for Students with Disabilities*. Baltimore, MD: Paul H. Brookes Publishing.

Giangreco, M. F. (2000) *Teaching Old Logs New Tricks: More Absurdities and Realities of Education*. Minnetonka, MN: Peytral Publications.

Gray, C. (1994a) *The Social Story Book*. Arlington, TX: Future Horizons.

Gray, C. (1994b) *Comic Strip Conversations*. Arlington, TX: Future Horizons.

Gray, C. (2002) *My Social Stories Book*. London: Jessica Kingsley.

Grove, N. and Walker, M. (1990) 'The Makaton Vocabulary: using manual signs and graphic symbols to develop interpersonal communication'. *Augmentative and Alternative Communication*, **6**, 15–28.

Howlin, P. and Rutter, M. (1987) *Treatment of Autistic Children*. London: Wiley.

Jones, G. (2002) *Educational Provision for Children with Autism and Asperger Syndrome*. London: David Fulton.

Kennard, G. K. (1992) *Signalong Phase 1 (Basic Vocabulary)*. Rochester: The Signalong Group.

Kennard, G. K. (1995a) *Signalong Foundation Course Training Pack*. Rochester: The Signalong Group (restricted availability).

Lewis, A. (2002) 'Accessing, through research interviews, the views of children with difficulties in learning', *Support For Learning*, **17**(3), 110–16.

National Literacy Strategy (2002) *Strand Tracker for Non-fiction Objectives*. London: DfES.

Newton, C. and Wilson, D. (1999) *Circles of Friends*. Dunstable: Folens.

Office for Standards in Education (2001) *Promoting and Evaluating Pupils' Spiritual, Moral, Social and Cultural Development*. London: Ofsted.

Office for Standards in Education (2003) *Handbook for Inspecting Secondary Schools*. London: Ofsted.

Office for Standards in Education (2003) *Special Educational Needs in the Mainstream*. London: Ofsted.

Park, K. (2003) 'A voice and a choice'. *Special Children*, **153**, Feb/March, 30–1.

Parker, M. (2000) 'Setting up a base for secondary age pupils with an autistic spectrum disorder within a mainstream school', *Good Autism Practice*, **1**(2), 62–70.

Qualifications and Curriculum Authority (2000) *A Scheme of Work for Key Stages 1 and 2: Music*. London: QCA.

Qualifications and Curriculum Authority (2000) *A Scheme of Work for History in Key Stages 1 and 2*. London: QCA.

Qualifications and Curriculum Authority (2001) *Planning, Teaching and Assessing the Curriculum for Pupils with Learning Difficulties*. London: QCA.

Qualifications and Curriculum Authority/ Department for Education and Skills (2001) *Supporting the Target Setting Process*. London: Department for Education and Employment.

Sainsbury, C. (2000) *Martian in the Playground*. Bristol: Lucky Duck Publishing.

Seach, D., Lloyd, M. and Preston, M. (2002*) Supporting Children with Autism in Mainstream Schools*. Birmingham: Questions Publishing.

Smith-Myles, B. and Simpson, R. L. (1998) *Asperger Syndrome: A Guide for Educators and Parents*. Austin, TX: Pro-Ed Publishing.

Tod, J. (1999) 'IEPs: Inclusive educational practices?'. *Support for Learning*, **14**(4), 184–8.

Walker, M., Davis, V. and Berger, A. (2002) *Tumpa Tumpa*. London: David Fulton.

Index

Accessibility Plans 1
adults 7, 31, 42, 45, 51, 53–4, 58, 60, 68, 73, 83, 92,
    97–8, 100–1, 104–7, 109, 111–13, 115, 117, 121,
    125–6, 134, 144
advocacy 66, 69
Annual Review 16–17, 27–8, 76, 88, 95, 120–1, 143
Antecedents, Behaviour and Consequences (abc) 98
anxiety 13–14, 19, 22, 29, 31, 49, 60, 97–8, 114,
    120, 133–4, 138, 141, 145
Asperger Syndrome 90
assessment 6, 11, 15, 20, 25, 35, 38, 43, 47, 49–50,
    54, 56, 73–4, 76, 79, 86, 98, 121–2, 136
Autistic Spectrum Disorders (ASD) 3, 13, 20, 23, 45,
    70, 112, 114–15

behaviour 17, 19–20, 22, 31, 34, 38, 41, 44, 49, 87,
    89–91, 93, 95, 97, 99–110, 133–4, 138–9, 141–2,
    145
body language 68, 105, 111, 115
Brain Gym 41, 140
British Sign Language 68, 114
buddies 58–9, 92, 107, 145
bullying 144

choices 28, 34, 45, 66, 70, 116–17, 123, 125, 128,
    144–5
Circle of Friends 58–60, 92, 107, 145
circle time 80, 120
citizenship 10
cloze procedure 48
clubs 68, 92, 115, 121, 145
comic strip conversations 126–7
communication 7, 11, 15–20, 22, 25, 27–9, 33, 37,
    41–2, 55, 61, 64–9, 71, 75, 84, 86–7, 90, 107,
    111–21, 125, 132, 143
comprehension 38, 45
computers 6, 46, 49, 69–70, 98
concept 6, 8–9, 14, 18, 78, 86, 118–19, 130, 137,
    139–41, 144
concept maps 6, 40, 130
context 16, 19, 34–5, 37–39, 45, 54, 62, 68, 75–8,
    81, 83, 89, 111, 125, 138
co-operative learning 93–4
curriculum 2, 5–8, 11, 16, 20, 25, 27, 30–4, 37–9,
    41, 43, 49–50, 53, 57, 60, 69, 74–6, 78–80, 83–4,
    87–8, 90, 95, 109, 119, 134, 136, 139, 142–4
    curriculum overlapping 37–8, 50

dictaphone 19, 47
differentiation 5–6, 31, 36
disability 1–4, 6–7, 9–11, 13, 15, 21–2, 24, 30, 32,
    74, 91, 95, 119–20
    disability awareness 21
Disability Discrimination Act (1995) 1, 10–11, 71,
    74

Disability Rights Commission 1, 3–4, 10, 74
diversity 5, 10, 30, 51, 91–2, 145
Down's Syndrome 9–10, 17, 20, 41
drama 33, 41, 86, 132

educational psychology 28, 59
educational psychologist 10–11, 24–5, 27, 59, 88,
    133, 143
emotions 7, 43, 87, 108, 123, 126, 132
entitlement 7, 37
expectations 5, 9, 14–15, 32, 39, 54, 58, 105, 135–6
experience 13–14, 25, 30, 38–9, 43, 49, 75–6, 78,
    81–6, 112, 121, 131
extra-curricular activities 2, 20, 68, 92
eye contact 44, 105, 111–12, 115, 126

facial expression 68, 83, 105–6, 123, 131
feelings 9, 14, 97–8, 101, 106, 108–9, 123, 126,
    128–32, 138
Foundation stage 30–1, 41, 60, 79, 134, 136
friends 14, 17, 58, 60, 79, 88, 91–2, 107, 121, 127,
    130–1

gesture 44, 68, 111, 113–14, 117, 121, 125, 132
governors 2, 4, 52, 58, 107
groups 31, 33, 35–7, 41–3, 47, 92–7, 138, 145

health and safety 10, 43
home–school diaries 17–18
homework 18–19, 45, 88

illness 4, 6, 20, 29, 80, 97, 106, 112
inclusion 1, 4–5, 7–10, 12, 14, 30–1, 38, 49–53, 58,
    73–4, 78, 90, 117, 132–3, 142, 144
independence 6, 16–17, 42, 55, 66, 69, 72, 82, 87,
    119, 123
Index for Inclusion 4, 51
Individual Behaviour Plans (IBP) 89
Individual Education Plans (IEP) 4, 19, 22, 26–7, 38,
    46, 49, 56–7, 71, 76, 79–80, 86–91
inference 44
information 2, 6, 10, 14–15, 17–20, 24, 27–8, 34–6,
    39–40, 42–4, 46, 51, 55–6, 62, 66, 70, 72, 76, 87,
    94–5, 103, 105, 109, 112, 117, 119, 121, 125,
    134–7
information technology 50
interaction 30–1, 55–6, 58, 91–3, 95, 106–7, 111,
    117, 127, 132, 136

jigsaw activities 93–5

key concepts 35–8, 50, 78, 144
Key Stage 1 24, 33, 41, 49, 78, 82
Key Stage 2 32–3, 39, 49, 77–8, 81–2, 111
kinaesthetic 39, 41, 95

language 7, 9, 15, 24–5, 37–8, 44, 48, 58, 61, 68, 79, 90–1, 111–12, 114–15, 119, 121, 123, 131, 136, 141, 143
laptop computers 46, 69
leadership 94
liaison 15, 56–7, 136, 142–3
   with Early Years settings 11
life skills 17, 23, 71, 145
literacy 7, 14, 17, 25, 33, 35, 37, 46, 61, 76–7, 87–8, 90, 102, 114, 119, 129, 139, 145
local education authorities (LEAs) 7, 10, 27, 71
lunchtime 115
   breaks 17
   supervisors 20, 55, 105

Makaton 68, 114
masks 128
medication 9, 11, 20–1, 60, 107
memory mats 66–7

National Curriculum 5–8, 31, 33, 37, 49, 74–9, 90
National Curriculum Inclusion Statement 5
National Literacy Strategy 77
numeracy 19, 33, 35, 37, 45, 76, 78, 81, 87, 139, 145

objectives 4–6, 25, 27, 33–35, 37, 47, 56, 75–8, 84
objects 6, 13, 30, 44, 48, 61–2, 64, 68, 75, 80, 84–5, 112, 115–17, 126
observations 49, 55
occupational therapy 11, 21, 25, 33, 72, 90
Office for Standards in Education (Ofsted) 9

P scales 11, 33, 35, 37, 49, 74–80, 83–4, 86, 90
pace 42
parents 1–2, 4, 6, 9, 11, 13–22, 24–30, 32–3, 44–6, 50, 87, 91–2, 97–8, 101, 106–7, 111, 120–1, 131
pastoral 28, 87
performance descriptions 74
personal care 9, 87
   toileting 9, 16, 23, 45, 116
Personal Social and Health Education (PSHE) 16, 35, 74, 92, 109
photographs 6, 18, 28, 40, 46, 49, 57, 61–5, 109, 112, 115–18, 123, 125, 128, 130–2, 134–5
physiotherapy 5, 33, 90, 141
Picture Exchange Communication System (PECS) 66
placements 2, 15, 17, 24, 51, 110, 135–6, 143, 145
planning 15–16, 18, 30–5, 37–9, 41–3, 49–50, 54–7, 60, 71–4, 76, 80–1, 88, 95, 120–1
play 17, 29–31, 41, 55, 58–9, 65, 70, 91, 97–8, 104–5, 107, 109, 134–7, 139
Primary National Strategy 75
problem solving 82–3
profound and multiple learning difficulties (PMLD) 83, 123
progress 5–6, 15, 20, 22, 26–7, 32–3, 38, 41, 46, 49, 54, 56, 60, 70, 76, 79–80, 86, 88–9, 136
   progression 62, 76–7, 79–83, 90

questionnaires 4, 123–4
questions 13, 15, 23, 25–7, 43–4, 48, 59, 80, 93–5, 117, 121, 125–6, 128, 130, 135

recording 34, 46–9, 52, 76
relationships 16, 29, 54, 79, 92–3, 138
reports 24, 27, 49, 54, 76, 79, 88
resources 5–7, 11, 32–4, 36–7, 40, 42, 47, 119, 136, 141
respite care 22
responsible body 2–3
risks 43, 82
rules 104, 140

scribe 47–8
self-esteem 9, 44–5, 133, 137
SEN and Disability Act 1
sensory cues 23, 43
sensory impairment 21, 41–2, 112
sequencing 47, 125
Signalong 68–9, 114, 136
signing 7, 11, 16, 44, 61–2, 68–9, 112, 114–15, 125, 136
social 4, 7–8, 19, 24, 31, 34, 74, 78, 80, 91–2, 102, 117, 135
social interaction 56, 90–1, 106
social services 25, 90
social skills 16, 25, 55, 73, 87, 91–2, 94, 106
social stories 7, 101–2, 109, 137
software 32, 37–8, 40, 46–7, 64, 66, 69–72, 87, 117, 119, 136
Special Educational Needs Code of Practice 14, 86–7, 90
Special Educational Needs Co-ordinator (SENCO) 11, 15, 27, 33, 37, 50, 87, 134
speech 19, 25, 58, 62, 68–9, 79, 90, 102–3, 111–14, 117, 119, 126, 128, 131, 136, 141
speech and language therapist 11, 25, 33, 58, 90–1, 142, 143
speech and language therapy 33, 90, 136, 141
spiritual, moral, social, and cultural development 91
statement of special educational needs 4, 27, 33, 72, 88
Statutory Assessment Tests (SATS) 49–50
strategies 1–2, 5–6, 10–12, 21–2, 34, 49, 54–6, 76, 86–7, 92–3, 102, 106, 111, 123
support 2, 4, 6, 8–10, 14–15, 18, 20–1, 23, 25, 31–2, 34, 39–40, 42, 47–8, 50–6, 58–62, 64–6, 68–9, 71–9, 81–2, 84, 86–90, 92, 94, 97, 102–3, 107, 111–12, 114–15, 117, 119, 121, 123, 125, 129–31, 133–4, 136–8, 142, 144–5
   peer 6, 50, 58, 73, 107, 145
   sensory 43, 50–1, 60
   visual 43, 50–1, 61, 65, 82, 140
support services 9, 90, 103, 143
switches 70–1
symbols 6, 11, 38–9, 42, 61–8, 71, 79, 82, 88, 94, 102, 104, 109, 112, 114–20, 123–5, 128, 130–1, 139–40
   communication boards 65–6, 117–18
   communication books 65–6, 117–18

targets 4, 6, 9, 16, 26–7, 32–3, 37–8, 46, 49, 57, 72, 74, 76, 78–80, 83, 87–90, 121
teaching assistants 2, 9–12, 14, 19–21, 24, 29, 32–3, 36–7, 42, 50–9, 63, 68, 72–3, 78, 83–4, 86–9, 95, 100, 104–5, 107, 111, 114, 117–18, 134–5, 137–8, 140, 142, 145
teaching strategies 5–6, 34, 87
teamwork 50
timetable 6, 18, 56, 59, 62, 65, 72, 116, 135, 140
tiredness 31, 106
tracking back 5, 33–5, 38, 50, 77–8, 81, 144
training 2, 4–5, 9–11, 20–1, 33, 52–5, 60, 68, 72, 105, 111, 114–15, 119, 136
transfer 14, 22, 39, 45, 49, 56, 70, 82, 112, 120, 130, 133–4, 136, 139, 142, 145
transition 14–15, 27, 34, 107, 132–6, 138, 140, 142–3, 145–6
transport 16, 22, 92
   to and from school 17

uniform 136

voice 13, 40, 68, 92, 110, 118, 120–1, 123, 132, 142

welcome 11, 20, 52
Widgit Software 64, 71, 119